EIGHT TALES

EIGHT TALES

by

CALEB GATTEGNO

Illustrated by Eve Rhind

EDUCATIONAL SOLUTIONS INC.
1974

ⓒ *C. Gattegno*
Translation by Ann Read
ISBN 0 87825 026 3

Originally published in Great Britain
by Educational Explorers Ltd.

Printing history
Educational Explorers edition published 1968
Educational Solutions Inc. edition published 1974

First American edition published by
EDUCATIONAL SOLUTIONS INC.
80 FIFTH AVENUE NEW YORK NY 10011

Made and printed in Great Britain by
Compton Printing Ltd, Aylesbury

CONTENTS

Princess Wadad and her friend Aly   7

Hassan the Short and Osman the Tall   17

The singing jugs   29

The white canary   43

The snail shell   67

The children in the clearing   77

Madcap in the clouds   87

The magic forest   99

PRINCESS WADAD AND HER FRIEND ALY

SULTAN SELIM in a fit of anger had dismissed his old friend the Emir Hussein from his palace. He had forbidden him and all his family to return to the capital and had ordered the soldiers not to allow him into the palace on pain of death.

At home on his estates, Emir Hussein was not the one who suffered most. He could go out hunting, go fishing, receive his friends and do a great many other things.

But Aly, his ten-year-old son, never stopped crying. Nothing was fun on his father's estates; he couldn't forget his games with Princess Wadad in the Sultan's palace, in that enormous room full of all the toys that they could want.

He kept on remembering her shrieks of laughter as she saw the piles of bricks so laboriously built up go tumbling down. In spite of the sadness in his heart, he couldn't hold back a smile at the thought of Wadad tripping over and upsetting all the little bricks as she fell, just when a whole house was nearly finished. Not a single brick had been left on top of another! And one of the bricks, a red one, had got stuck in her nose and looked like blood flowing. How frightened he had been! But how he had laughed when he saw what had really happened! Wadad didn't see that her fall and the collapse of the building were all that funny, and was inclined to be cross. Aly tried to explain, but it was no use: he couldn't speak for laughing.

So he flung himself down on the floor and put the red brick under his nose, with a corner pushed into his nostril, and it was Wadad's turn to laugh. They made such a noise that the faithful servant Asma came to see what was happening. Seeing Aly in that position, she thought he was hurt and called for help while the children laughed all the harder. Then Asma saw and laughed too; the whole palace re-echoed with their mirth.

Aly remembered so many things that he could no longer bear to be apart from Wadad. He decided that he would go back to the palace, to her. At night in bed, instead of sleeping, he made plans for his journey. He would do such and such, he would take so much bread, a particular bag, wear certain clothes and take his stick; but he would have to leave his dog behind.

The thought of leaving gave him an appetite and everybody thought he had got over his unhappiness at last. He ate his meals and ran about all over the garden.

But one morning, very early, Aly left his father's house. He went a way he knew well, where no-one would see him, and soon he was on the road to the palace, a road he had travelled so many times with his father and his servants.

He had to walk quickly across streams and through woods, for he didn't want it to be dark before he reached the palace.

Luckily, on the way he met some merchants on horseback who were riding towards the town. He begged them to take him with them and offered them the bread that he had with him. The merchants were sorry for him, set him on a horse and gave him some figs and nuts which they were carrying.

Aly was all smiles. The merchants, seeing him so pleased, thought it was because of the figs and gave him some more. But he was happy because he was going back to see his friend and play with her again. Suddenly he stopped eating and thought to himself: "I must keep some of these in case Wadad wants some." And he put the rest in his bag.

* * *

It was dusk when they came to the town and lamps were

8

already being lit in the houses. Near the palace, Aly said goodbye to the merchants, thanked them, and prayed that God would protect them always.

When they had gone he made his way to the main entrance of the palace. It was closed and two soldiers stood guard there, two tall Africans with swords and lances. The only light came from two lanterns at their feet. Aly told them that he wanted to see the princess. In answer the guards levelled the points of their lances at him, indicating that it would be the worse for him if he didn't go away. Then he told them he was the Emir's son and the princess's great friend. The soldiers began to laugh and walked towards him. Aly ran off.

He went down one street and back up another. The soldiers didn't notice that he had returned. He picked up two pebbles and crash, crash, he threw them at the lanterns and broke the glass. The wind blew them out.

The guards panicked and didn't know what to do. Aly threw another pebble at a window opposite the gate and broke a pane. The soldiers ran to see what was going on: Aly rushed to the gate, pushed it open and was in the palace courtyard.

Just then other soldiers came running towards the gateway and if Aly hadn't flattened himself against a wall they would have run into him. And there he had to stay for more than an hour while the soldiers were busy looking for the person who had broken the pane of glass.

But gradually all became quiet again. The sentries' lanterns were replaced and the other soldiers went back to the guard-room.

Aly crept quietly along the wall in the darkness. His heart was beating fast and he didn't know if he would be able to find Wadad with all those men on watch. Besides, there was a little moonlight and the sentries he could see going their rounds would spot him and take him away. He was far from happy. But he so much wanted to see Wadad!

Slipping along the wall, Aly came to a place where the ground was covered with small pebbles which crunched under his feet. After every step he had to wait with beating heart till the noise had had time to be forgotten. He was making such slow progress that he thought it would be daylight before he found the stairs.

Luckily he came to another stretch which was lighter and more even. He walked quickly, he almost ran. But he had to stop very suddenly as two sentries approached. He thought they had seen him and were going to catch him, but they went by without noticing him.

What a fright it gave him! His forehead was covered with cold sweat.

But he pulled himself together. There was Wadad's room in front of him, on the second floor. He had only to cross the courtyard and go in through the doorway. Ah, but the whole court was moonlit; if he ran across it, someone would be sure to see him.

So he had to crawl, crouching down with his bag over his head to make himself the same colour as the ground. Silently he crept along, like a tortoise, slowly, slowly. And once more Providence came to his aid: he reached the door that led upstairs without being seen.

But this time he very nearly was caught, for the sentries were standing talking on the stairs. He would never be able to distract their attention and get past.

He was on the point of tears when he felt a rainwater pipe under his hand. He had an idea. He would climb up the pipe to the balcony of Wadad's room.

So up he went, climbing like a monkey up a tree, hanging on to every hole in the wall, hurting himself, using hands and feet. In the midst of his efforts he heard the sentries' steps as they made their round of the courtyard, coming towards him.

They seemed to be looking at him, about to shout at him; he could see them coming nearer and nearer.

Clinging to a bar, Aly thought he would fall, so weak did he feel. Just as the soldiers got to the foot of the wall, he saw them turn in through the gate and he breathed again.

Just one more effort and there he was on the balcony of Wadad's room. He looked all round.

Everything was quiet.

He tapped lightly on the shutter. Nobody answered. He tapped again, but still lightly. Still nothing. He tapped a little harder.

He heard Wadad's voice calling in alarm: "Asma! Asma! Someone's knocking at the window. I'm frightened!"

Aly called out: "Wadad, Wadad, it's me, your friend Aly."

Fortunately, Asma hadn't woken up.

Wadad ran to the shutter, opened it and let Aly in without anyone hearing.

"Aly, Aly, how pleased I am to see you again! I was sure you'd come back; I knew you wouldn't leave me here to be bored all on my own," she said, kissing him.

Aly, seeing Asma lying near the foot of the bed, put his finger to his lips and drew Wadad into the next room, which was the playroom. He turned up the lamp and while Wadad stared at him joyfully, he looked round.

★   ★   ★

Everything was the same. All the toys were in their places. He recognised everything. Over there were the dolls, broken ones and new ones, rag dolls and wooden ones. The clothes that they had so often dressed them in were there too, piled up higgledy-piggledy in a corner.

They hadn't played with the dolls for a long time. There were so many more interesting things! Those three wooden horses, one on wheels and two rocking horses; what fun they had had with them, how many times had they nearly broken their necks falling off! Those horses had been given to Wadad by the head of the town's Guild of Carpenters who had made them specially for her.

Indeed all Wadad's toys had been made just for her. The yacht that she sailed on the pool in summer was so beautiful that whenever Aly dreamed of travelling, he wanted it to be on a boat like that. It was big and so well-made that when it sailed off over the water it could carry all Wadad's little dolls and go a long way without ever capsizing. In summer there was nothing they had liked more than playing with the yacht.

As his gaze travelled all round the room, Aly recalled the games they had played with each toy and joyfully remembered all those happy days. But irresistibly his eyes went back towards the middle of the room where the bricks for the building game that had absorbed them so many weeks ago still lay in a heap.

There were hundreds and hundreds of bricks painted in the brightest colours and in the boxes at the side there were iron gates and tiny lanterns that could really be lit, beams and tiles and everything for building houses, palaces and stables.

Aly could wait no longer; he flung himself onto the pile and began to build up the bricks so fast and so well that Wadad soon saw he was making her own palace, the one she lived in.

She watched in admiration. She recognised everything: the main entrance, the balconies, the courtyards, the walls; and every time Aly added another little brick she shouted "Lovely!" and clapped her hands.

But Aly hadn't finished. In the boxes of soldiers he found some sentries and placed them at the doors, in the courtyard, in the guardroom and in front of the gateway. Then he picked up a little toy man and took him through all the movements that he himself had made in the courtyard. Wadad watched him fascinated and when she saw Aly making the little man climb up the water pipe and tap at her shutter, she realised that he was

13

telling her of his own adventure; she flung her arms round his neck and kissed him and said how much she loved him, he was so fine and brave.

But Aly hadn't finished yet. He took a little wax doll and put it in Wadad's room; he opened the shutter and brought the little Aly doll into the room where he had put an Asma at the foot of the bed; then he took the two dolls into the next room. There, there were some building bricks and the little Aly was just going to begin making another palace when they heard Asma's voice. She was calling.

The real Asma. She was looking for Wadad.

But Wadad wanted to hide Aly, thinking that Asma would go and tell her father that her friend was there, and she was afraid. She kept quiet and Asma called more and more loudly. Asma saw the open shutter and, thinking the little girl had gone out that way, ran out calling. In the courtyard the guards heard her. The sun had been up a long time. The guards ran up and down the staircases calling "Wadad, Princess Wadad!" All the noise awoke the Sultan and his wife, Wadad's mother. They were alarmed and ran out in their dressing-gowns to look for their daughter.

They looked everywhere. Everyone shouted, but Wadad pressed close to Aly and still made no sound.

When they had searched throughout the palace for an hour, the Sultan and his wife came to their daughter's room weeping. "Ah heavens! My daughter has vanished. Where is she? Who will bring her back to me? Who can tell me where she has gone? I will give half my kingdom to whoever finds her."

And the Sultan wept and wept and Wadad stayed silent, with her hand over Aly's mouth because he wanted to call out.

The Sultan wanted to see the toys with which his beloved daughter had played; he opened the playroom and saw her with Aly. Wadad was dumb with fright.

14

The Sultan rushed over and took her in his arms, kissing her and shouting with joy; everybody came into the playroom, praising God for restoring Wadad to her father.

But after a few minutes the Sultan noticed Aly.

"Ah, it's you, you rascal, who would have stolen my daughter! It's your fault I've suffered so much, thinking she was dead. You shall pay for that." He rushed to seize him by the scruff of the neck. But Wadad shouted so loudly that he stopped and turned to her. "What's the matter? Have I hurt you? You're not going to stop me punishing this wicked boy who has come here though I forbade it, and who kept quiet while everyone was calling you?"

"Father, father, it isn't his fault. He wanted to shout out, but I stopped him. I was afraid you'd hurt him because he came here in spite of you. But if you say you love me and are glad to have me back, forgive him; he's my friend and he's so good and brave. Look, he came here alone all the way from his home; he got past all the sentries and climbed right up here."—"Do you call that good and brave," the Sultan answered, "to behave like a robber, coming in where he's forbidden to come, climbing pipes? I'll have him punished straight away. Put him in prison!"

The soldiers were just seizing Aly when Wadad interrupted again. "But, father, he's my friend. Is it his fault if his father displeased you? I like him; he's the only boy I can play with; he's so clever that he makes all my toys interesting. Look at those building bricks. Look what he's made and see how good it is."

The Sultan turned round and recognised his palace. "What! Was it you, Aly, who made that?"—"Yes father, it was Aly, and he knows how to make a lot more things; if you like he'll show you." Then the Sultan took Aly by one hand and Wadad by the other and took them to his room. Everyone else stayed in the playroom. They admired Aly's palace and couldn't believe that he had made it.

★　★　★

Meanwhile Aly's father was looking everywhere for him, in the woods and by the rivers. He was very worried.

★　　★　　★

Wadad asked the Sultan if she could keep Aly with her always.

The Sultan thought for a few moments, then called a vizier. "Go to Emir Hussein and tell him that his son Aly is here, that I'm keeping him and that I want the Emir to come and live in the palace with me."

Two days later there was a great celebration at the palace. Emir Hussein came and they told him that Aly was to be betrothed to Wadad; and that they would be married when they were eighteen. The Sultan forgave the Emir because of his son, who was such a fine boy.

For eight years Aly and Wadad played and studied together. Aly became a builder of palaces, roads and bridges. Wadad grew into the most beautiful princess in the world.

For their wedding there was a magnificent feast; ten thousand people were invited and it has always been said that Aly and Wadad lived happily ever after.

HASSAN THE SHORT AND OSMAN THE TALL

IN A STREET in Basra exactly opposite each other, there were two big shops where you could buy the most beautiful things.

When a lady went into one, the owner of the other was annoyed. But since the two rivals, Hag Moussa and Ahmed Effendi, sold precisely the same goods, the people of Basra went to one or other of the shops according to which shopkeeper they liked best.

In many people's eyes, the shops differed only in the colour of the paint on their walls, since you could get the same materials, the same jewellery and the same slippers in both.

One day Hag Moussa called his son Hassan and said to him: "Hassan, I have called you the Short ever since your body stopped growing, but you know how much I value your intelligence. So I trust you with the task of going to Baghdad to get me some jewels that Ahmed Effendi doesn't know of. I've had enough of seeing customers go to that shopkeeper rather than coming to me, when he hasn't even deserved the Lord's help by making the journey to Mecca. You must bring me back some jewels that are rare in value and in quality. Here are ten thousand pieces of gold. Mind you don't get robbed."

Hassan, not wanting to attract the attention of Ahmed Effendi's men, arranged to meet his servants and his caravan at the north gate of the town at dawn on the following day.

★   ★   ★

The journey was uneventful and Hassan arrived safely in

17

Baghdad about midday a few days later.

He asked to see the jewellers. But he didn't like anything they had. He wanted some really fine pearls.

A salesman offered to take him, for one piece of silver, to a merchant who sold pearls of the purest sort.

Through streets that got narrower and narrower, he led him to a doorway so low that you had to bend double to go through.

Once inside the house, Hassan could scarcely stand upright, short as he was, and his turban brushed against the ceiling and got covered with whitewash.

He called three times: "Si Fathi, Si Fathi, Si Fathi!" just as the salesman had told him to do if he wanted to make his presence known.

After a few minutes' silence, he felt something tug at his robe. Thinking that it was some animal, he bent down to shoo it away, but his hand was seized, and with his forefinger he brought before his eyes a little man no bigger than your hand.

Hassan was so astonished that he didn't listen to a voice that was scarcely audible. Taking out of his pocket a big magnifying glass which was to be a present for his grandfather, he examined Si Fathi, for Si Fathi it was.

He was exactly like anybody else; he even wore metal-framed spectacles and had one gold tooth. His beard was grey and his head almost bald. In the belt of his navy blue silk robe he carried threads of every conceivable colour, and some scissors.

When Hassan had finished examining him he noticed that Si Fathi's lips were moving and he put him close to his ear to hear what he was saying.

"What do you want? You've come here disturbing me and you're hurting me squeezing me between your fingers; put me down and tell me quickly what you want, because I've got a lot to do."

Hassan, fearing that his voice would be too much for Si Fathi's ears, put his handkerchief over his mouth to soften the force of his breath and said, "Si Fathi, greetings to you from myself and from my father, Hag Moussa of Basra. My father, who is a jeweller, has commissioned me to buy him the finest pearls in Baghdad and I've been told that you sell them."

Si Fathi, standing on Hassan's shoulder, spoke directly into his ear: "Pick up your magnifying glass and look in the corner over on the left. What can you see?"

"I can see insects going to and fro among a lot of colours."

"Look again," said Si Fathi.

Hassan went nearer and saw that the insects were nothing less than very little men, as big as a finger joint, and that the colours were threads and pearls, and that the threads were being threaded through the pearls faster than the eye could follow.

Hassan asked in wonderment who the workmen were. Si Fathi told him that they were three of his children by his last wife, who was in the garden asleep in a rose. They were only eight, nine and ten years old, but they had learned to work so well that they could thread pearls for hours on end without stopping.

Hassan had another question: "Who buys such tiny pearls and what use are they?"

Si Fathi showed him a bottle and said: "When the pearls are threaded into necklaces I dip them into this bottle which contains a wonderful liquid. Then any woman or girl who puts one of these necklaces round her neck sees her face become as beautiful as the full moon."

Hassan realised at once that the necklaces would delight all the women of Basra and that nobody would go to Ahmed Effendi's shop any more. He could hardly contain himself for joy, and asked how much the bottle and ten thousand necklaces would cost. Si Fathi answered that he never sold anything but the pearls and the thread. But Hassan objected that he wouldn't find any-body to make up necklaces out of them. He asked the price of some pearls, thread, the bottle and one of the workmen. Si Fathi refused the suggestion, but when he heard Hassan mention two thousand gold pieces, he granted his youngest son Ali to the merchant from Basra.

Ali was put in a box, in which Hassan had made some air holes with a pin. Into a handkerchief he put the pearls and thread; and the precious bottle, inside a tin box, was placed in the pocket where he carried his money, near his heart, in the shirt he wore next to his skin.

Without waiting any longer, Hassan set off on horseback for Basra, leaving his caravan and taking his servants with him to protect his precious charge from robbers.

★　　★　　★

As soon as he arrived he ran joyfully to his father. But he, expecting to see a caravan appear such as would make his neighbour jealous, was very disappointed.

"What, my son! Did you go to Baghdad for fun, or to buy goods? Where's the caravan? Tell me quickly what you've been doing for so long and so far from home."

Hag Moussa rushed on and on and Hassan, pleased to think of the surprise he had for him, smiled and smiled, which annoyed his father even more. Hag Moussa even started to threaten him and if meanwhile Hassan hadn't spread out his handkerchief on the table and placed Ali in the centre, and if he hadn't gently invited his father to look through the magnifying glass, the paternal cane would have come into play.

Hag Moussa refused to look, but his son's words had calmed him a little and he said:

"What are you up to? Have you gone mad? Did I send you so far for knick-knacks like that? And how much did you pay for those trifles?"

"Two thousand pieces of gold."

"Two thousand pieces of gold! Good Lord help us! My son, my only son has lost his reason and will make me lose mine next."

He would have become even angrier, but his son, still smiling, begged him to glance through the magnifying glass. Hag Moussa tried, but tears of rage blurred his vision. He dried his eyes and, still angry, had a look.

Completely amazed to see such a tiny fellow working so perfectly, he was almost ready to pardon his son's stupidity when Hassan, with a pair of tweezers, picked up one of the necklaces that Ali had just finished, dipped it into the bottle and, calling an ugly beggar-girl who was moaning at the door, put it round her neck.

The girl who had been so ugly became in a flash as beautiful as the light of day and Hag Moussa wept for joy. He couldn't congratulate his son enough and praised God for having given him such intelligence.

In a moment all Basra heard that Hassan had just brought back from Baghdad very fine necklaces that would transform any woman's face and make her beautiful. Hag Moussa's shop was immediately invaded by all the women in Basra.

Each necklace was sold for a hundred silver pieces and all the women of Basra wanted to have several in reserve. They were so fine that they broke very easily.

For a month nobody bought anything at all from Ahmed Effendi, because the same things could be got opposite and there was always the sight of some charming transformation.

Hag Moussa was doubly satisfied: he was selling a lot and his rival was selling nothing at all. Every day he blessed Hassan and stroked Ali—and didn't forget to praise God.

Ali and Hassan had become great friends and used to talk to each other when work was over, with Ali sitting on the edge of Hassan's ear and Hassan with a handkerchief over his mouth.

★   ★   ★

Ahmed Effendi was very unhappy and didn't know how to attract the people of Basra. It was no use his rearranging his displays or stationing criers at the door or announcing substantial reductions in his prices. Nothing did any good.

One evening in despair he asked for his son's assistance.

"Osman, God made you tall and strong; can you not help me in some way?"

"Listen, father, I was told by a traveller at the harbour that in Teheran there are very clever artists who make materials more beautiful than any that have ever been seen. Why shouldn't I go and get you some?"

Ahmed Effendi gave him ten tousand pieces of gold and his blessing.

Osman got ready a caravan and went to Teheran.

There he searched for a long time for new materials, but nothing was to his liking. The finest of those materials wouldn't win back the lost trade in Basra.

He had been there a fortnight and he was very sadly deciding to go home when, taking a last stroll through the streets of the town, he heard a craftsman mentioned who made materials that were sought after by kings.

Osman went to see the craftsman and tried his luck.

He was very well received and was given a cup of coffee in a golden cup. The craftsman must have been very rich. His name was Jabir and he had travelled a great deal. For some years he had lived a few miles from Teheran and people came to him if they wanted a rich piece of material.

Osman told Jabir of his disappointment in Teheran and begged him to show him his richest materials.

Jabir brought him a piece of stuff that he had made for the new wife of the king of Turkestan. It was really beautiful and when looked at from different angles it appeared different colours; next to the skin it became transparent.

Osman greatly admired it but wondered what effect it would have on the Basra public, who knew Hassan's necklaces.

Remembering his deserted shop, Osman turned pale and Jabir asked him if he felt unwell. Osman told him the whole story of the necklaces and how upset he was at the idea of going back to Basra without having found anything more beautiful to compete with them.

Jabir left him for a moment and came back with a piece of material the size of a tablecloth. Then he said:

"You see this piece of material; it's small, but if you cut a piece and stretch it all ways, you can make a whole dress out of it."

With his scissors, he cut a piece three fingers wide and stretched it. The material grew and spread and Jabir asked Osman to think of a colour and a design. And a beautiful green dress appeared a second later in Jabir's hands. Osman clapped his hands and danced for joy.

Jabir told him how a princess he had known in his youth had ordered that marvellous material from him, but she had never come to claim it. He would gladly give it to Osman, for whom he felt a liking, if he would pay him the five thousand pieces of gold which was the price of the things he had used in making it.

Jabir added that the material had the power of transforming the body of whoever wore it.

Osman said to himself that if the necklaces made people more beautiful, it was only their faces: they didn't alter the body, and he could already imagine how many transformations his arrival in Basra would cause.

Osman paid Jabir the required sum, thanked him and set off at once.

His journey back was made practically without a stop. Osman carried the precious material under his shirt, and his heart beat more loudly in his breast than his horses' hooves on the road.

★   ★   ★

His father waited for him every evening in the deserted shop. Nobody came to him any more. At Hag Moussa's shop crowds of women and girls were coming and going all the time.

When Ahmed Effendi saw Osman coming he ran to meet him. Although he could see no caravan, he wasn't angry. He remembered Hassan's arrival with the necklaces, and he asked his son to tell him quickly all that he had done.

Osman said not a word, but brought out the material from under his shirt and with his father's scissors cut off a small piece. He stretched it out all ways and thought of the colour sky blue. Then Osman threw it over his father, and Ahmed Effendi became slim and elegant like a young man of twenty. His large stomach disappeared, his body became like an athlete's, and Osman laughed to see his father so handsome.

Ahmed Effendi looked at himself in the mirror and knew that all Basra would be in his shop next day.

On the following morning, Osman and his father went out into the streets of Basra, one with a drum and the other carrying pieces of the precious material on a black velvet cushion.

When they reached the residential districts, Osman beat his drum and his father cried out:

"Who wants to be made beautiful for a hundred gold pieces?"

And the ladies and their daughters came to him and looked.

Osman asked how they would like their figures to be and what colour they wanted to wear, and in a few seconds the dress was finished and the wearer transformed.

Oh, the number of girls who were made happy that day!

In Basra there was already no-one left with an ugly face; now all their bodies could be made beautiful and Basra was to become the town of the most beautiful women in the world.

That evening Osman said to his father: "Now there's no need for us to go out any more: customers will flock to us."

In the morning, as soon as it was dawn, people were knocking at the door of Ahmed Effendi's shop, asking for some of the new material.

Nobody set foot in Hag Moussa's shop that day.

★   ★   ★

And the days went by. Ahmed Effendi's trade flourished and Hag Moussa bewailed his lot.

He called Hassan: "Do something!" he said.

Hassan went out and crossed over towards the shop opposite. He called Osman, who came out to him with a triumphant smile.

"Well then," he said, "you thought you were going to beat me. What do you say now?"

Hassan looked at him and said:

"I suggest that we go into partnership; you have the material and I the necklaces; together we could do wonders. Why try to harm each other?"

Osman replied with a laugh:

"Why didn't you come to me with that suggestion when you came back from Baghdad?"

"Because my father was the owner of the shop, but since then he has handed over to me."

"Well, my father has handed over his shop to me, too, and I refuse."

"What's the use of being obstinate? You are clever and so am I; we shall do better business if we go into partnership."

"No," replied Osman curtly. "I intend to punish you for all the trouble I had in Teheran. If you go on annoying me it will be the worse for you."

While he was saying all this, Hassan murmured to Ali who lay in his ear. Ali ran up Osman's robe, climbed onto his head and got into his eye. He began to jig up and down so hard that Osman begged Hassan to come to his aid. But Hassan refused unless he agreed to the partnership. Osman, blinded by tears, promised, and Hassan took Ali and put him back in his usual place.

Osman was crying like a child. He realised that it isn't always enough to be the biggest in order to be right.

Two days later the new partners had drawn up plans for building a very large shop.

When it was open the two fathers, the former rivals, received the customers together. The two sons went off, each his own way, and brought back objects of greater and greater rarity and value.

Their shop was talked of in all the important towns and people came from far away for the most beautiful jewels and the richest materials.

A few years later, Hassan's sister married Osman and they had a son. He was called Fathi, in memory of the maker of the pearl necklaces which had been the beginning of their great fortune.

But Hassan didn't marry: he was too short. No rich woman in Basra would have him, in spite of the elegance that Osman's material gave him. Osman had no other children and Fathi looked after the shop when his parents grew old.

THE SINGING JUGS

In his cottage at the top of a steep slope, Bassiri had been making jugs for twenty years and going every Friday to sell them in the neighbouring villages. The potter's wheel stood in a corner of the only room in the house, right under one of the two skylights through which the bright light from outside filtered softly. Bassiri loved working at his wheel and he made up songs to enliven the routine of his work.

He had built his cottage himself, out of the same good clay that he now used for making his jugs. It had only taken a few days. His craft he had learned in his native village, which he had left after a quarrel with his father. In spite of his affection for his mother and sisters, Bassiri had decided to settle for good in this other village where once he had sold his father's jugs, and whose good soil he had liked.

For his home he had chosen a remote and peaceful spot, accessible only by means of a stony path and exposed all round to the wind and sun. The villagers had watched in silence while he built it and he hadn't asked them for anything. It was obvious that he was a master of his art and he seemed happy to use his strength and knowledge in that occupation.

His new house was strangely like the one he had just left, but very different from the others in the village. Bassiri had worked on it from dawn till dusk, only stopping for a short time to have his meal, which was always the same. From his bag, Bassiri would take a piece of the flat dry maize bread which the peasants of the district baked once a week. He used to brighten his meal with a bit of goat's milk cheese, fermented and sharp-tasting, the sort that stings your palate and makes you very thirsty. His large water bottle, which he filled at the village fountain, was scarcely enough to last him the day. Several times a day he poured out a good jugful, into a jug of which he was particularly fond because it kept the water cooler than any other. It was one of the first that his father had allowed him to make and for years it had seemed as if nothing could break it.

When the house was finished, Bassiri had gone into the town and brought back a potter's wheel which he placed, like his father's, to the right of the doorway, under the skylight where it was cool and there was enough light. Other essentials appeared one by one and the cottage looked more and more like the house he had left.

On the other side of the room he spread some straw to make a bed. In the centre he put a mat and a low stool where he could have his meals. Just opposite the door, against the wall, there stood a table and a stove to cook on.

Bassiri's plans were quite clear. He was going to take a wife and have a family. He had to make up his mind whether it was to be a girl from his own village, or from the one where he now lived. He quickly realised that he would have a better choice in the village where his home now was; so he went to see the most venerable of the old men there and told him what he wanted. The old man had already seen that Bassiri was hardworking and skilled. Now he could see too that he was a fine-looking man and very well-mannered. He asked him, however, how much money he had, as that would show his ambitions. Bassiri had a few pieces of gold and his first stock of jugs, which he was to sell soon in the neighbourhood. Then the old man told him that he would see the parents of a girl whom he knew to be good, capable and even pretty.

A few weeks later Fatma came to live with her husband. The

ritual of the wedding celebrations had been observed and the whole village had taken part. Bassiri was accepted into the community to live like everyone else there. His wife would be acknowledged and respected. For her part, she was happy that her parents had married her to the only man in the village who came from elsewhere, and whom in her heart she had wanted ever since the first day she saw him.

In this happy, busy household, Afzal, the hero of our story, was born.

*　　*　　*

Fatma had no other children. Afzal took up all her time, and Bassiri's greatest pleasure was to watch the two of them.

Slowly, as the child grew up and learned about life, Bassiri planned his son's future. Their kiln had been made bigger and they now burned more maize stalks in it, which made the firing of the jugs better. Bassiri invented jugs of new shapes and his market for them increased in size and variety.

When Afzal was big enough to carry a jug he went with his father to the next village. When he could carry a basket and several jugs he explored a wider area. And thus Afzal grew up to be like his father, strong and hardworking, with a very good understanding of what was liked by the customers in the different districts. The two of them by themselves managed to produce and deliver enough jugs every few weeks for the customers of the whole area.

It was a happy household. Afzal was now eighteen and his mother, with an eye to his future, was considering her neighbours and their daughters. She mentioned the matter to her husband and together they talked for a long time of the various merits of the girls among whom their son might find a wife. But finding a suitable girl wasn't the only problem. The question of where they would live arose, and neither of them could bear the idea of Afzal going to live somewhere away from them. The most attractive plan was to build another hut like their own for the newly married couple, on the same ground, on the far side of the kiln.

Unfortunately, while making one of his rounds in a distant town, Bassiri met with an accident and never came home again. Fatma and Afzal were long inconsolable, but found some distraction in the work that had accumulated. They now had to satisfy the needs of the same customers with only the young man's resources and what little help his unskilled mother could give.

Afzal's weariness began to show in his whole body. He had become thin and hollow-cheeked. In the village, the girls who had admired him from behind their closed shutters and wished he was their husband, now began to find fault with him. His cap no longer sat sideways on his head, giving him the swagger that they loved. His belt was often forgotten and his robe, which had always been a brilliant white, was now stained. His walk was no longer the lively step of a young gallant aware of the looks that followed his progress from darkened, closed rooms. Suddenly he had become a family's bread-winner and was consequently less eligible.

Afzal thought little about himself. He was too used to his father's punctuality and dared not refuse work. Yet he was losing customers, either because of delays or because of faults in his products. The weight of responsibility that lay on him was so great that he could no longer reconcile the number of orders received with the need to uphold his father's reputation.

One day he was carrying a basket of jugs on his head through the streets of a town when he passed by the house of a rich merchant who was celebrating some event with liberal supplies of wine. One of the guests, standing behind the gate outside the house, addressed Afzal as he went by, in thick drunken tones:

"If you were to mix my powdered bones with your clay, you could make jugs that sing."

Having tossed this remark at Afzal, he burst out laughing and went back into the house.

The poor young man stood amazed. Whatever did the man mean? Why provoke him like that? What was that about singing jugs and powdered bones?

Instead of going on his way through the town to sell the jugs he was carrying, Afzal went home and lay down on his bed. It was the first time he had ever done so and his mother thought he must be ill. To all her questions, he refused to answer except by sighs.

All through the night, Afzal lay wide awake in the dark, hearing the cursed remark that had assumed torturing proportions. He kept seeing himself killing the man and cutting out his bones, like a butcher, to grind them up. And the vision tormented him horribly.

"What did the man mean? Why should he torture me? Is it true that there can be jugs that sing?"

The idea consoled him a little. He would be the first to make jugs that sang when anyone drank from them. He would make them in a particular style for children drinking water and in a different style for princes and potentates who drink wine in spite of the Prophet's command; he would colour and decorate them to make them even more attractive. He would become more famous than his father and be admired everywhere. He would be rich, and would marry an elegant girl from the city.

But to make such jugs he would have to commit a murder. Not for a single moment had Afzal done anything but work and love, all his life. He had served great and humble people, poor and rich, masters and servants, with equal care and equal desire to please, as his father had taught him. But now that his father was dead and people seemed to take him for a good-for-nothing

trickster, would he be capable of the worst? His head spun. His eyes were glazed. Fantasies crowded one upon the other, each more painful than the last. He could have screamed—but the presence of his mother at his side forced him to be silent.

Fatma hadn't slept all night. She had watched over her son, hoping to hear regular breathing to tell her he was sleeping. But in the morning she could see he hadn't moved; his eyes were open and his lips tense. Should she question him? She did not dare. She got up and made a meal, but even then she dared not disturb him to give it to him. For her too it was a new experience, one of anxiety and mystery.

Afzal remained in the same state right through the day. "He's still alive," thought his mother, "because he watches me now and then. But he is terribly worried. There's something behind it all. Is it delayed shock at his father's death? Is it tiredness? Is it our poverty?" She could hardly accept any of these explanations, as Afzal had always confided his troubles and worries to her. What could it be?

Night descended again on the gloomy, silent house. Afzal still hadn't moved and Fatma had gone on wondering in vain. They both lay in their beds, though they were wide awake, and endlessly thought over the same questions without finding any answers, he trying to put away the temptation to commit murder, she dwelling on her helplessness in the face of a misfortune greater than she had ever known.

*   *   *

A ray of light entered Fatma's thoughts when she invoked Bassiri's name and appealed for his help. She relived the conversations she had had with her husband on the subject of Afzal's marriage. He had often said: "That boy is grown up now. He needs a wife."

"Yes, that must be it," said Fatma to herself, "he needs a wife.

35

That's what's causing all the trouble. I'll go to the village and find him one tomorrow." And with a smile, she fell asleep to dream of all the girls in the village. But he meanwhile continued his struggle with the torturing visions.

★   ★   ★

Early in the morning Fatma went off to see her neighbours.

Om Jabir was standing at her door watching a hen and her chickens. She had three marriageable daughters and was all sweetness towards Fatma. When she saw her coming she ran to meet her.

"How is your son, Om Afzal? I didn't see him all day yesterday. I hope he isn't ill? May Allah preserve him and give him strength."

"Don't worry, he's all right. He wanted a little rest. He has worked too hard since his poor father's death. But tell me, Om Jabir, how are your daughters?"

An interest in her daughters was exactly what Om Jabir failed to evoke in the mothers who had a son to marry off. Now that she had one within reach, she made the most of it.

"My eldest is like a dream, as beautiful as the full moon. Her hair is a cascade of ebony; she has the grace of a gazelle and the hands of a fairy. The next is as sweet as honey and as elegant as a dragon-fly, all fire and high spirits. My youngest has no equal but her sisters, and is known for her modesty, which will find favour in your eyes. Om Afzal, you wouldn't find anywhere for your son a more careful housewife or a more beautiful and attentive wife to bear his children."

Fatma was silent at this torrent of praises. If they were really like their mother said, which one should she choose? She ventured to ask how much of the property would go to each of the daughters.

Om Jabir, whose son Jabir was her favourite, still hoped to be able to marry off her daughters without taking any of the inheritance from their brother. She stammered something incomprehensible, but in tones that were enough to send Fatma away—her education in the processes of making marriage bargains hadn't been neglected. She said she would come back, and went off.

At Om Omar's she found the daughter of the house busy grinding pepper. A strong smell of spices greeted her and made her sneeze several times. The girl was buxom and gay; her bare legs gripped the mortar. Fatma liked her and imagined her working at her house, smiling and lovable; she would be able to rouse her son and make him forget his worries. Their conversation came straight to the point. The girl asked if Afzal wanted to get married. She claimed that she liked him a lot but was hoping that her parents would choose for her the next-door-neighbour's son, who was tall and dark; he worked in the town and came home very late every evening.

Fatma didn't listen to any more and didn't try to see Om Omar. A bit put out by the boldness of the little village girl, she went right to the other end of the village to see Om Hafiz, the fortune-teller. Fatma didn't want to tell anybody anything, but she was so worried that she asked Om Hafiz if she could tell her whom her son should marry.

She was answered in these words: "He will marry the girl who can capture his heart and who will give him hers, and who will reveal to him all the deepest secrets of the tombs." Fatma didn't understand but dared not ask for explanations. She went back home to her son.

★ ★ ★

Afzal had got up and, pale and weak, was walking towards his wheel, where the clay was lying covered with a damp cloth. His mother appeared at the doorway and went up to him.

"You know, Afzal, how much your father wanted you to

marry. Will you choose one of the girls from the village? I will make a fine wedding feast for you, and you shall have lots of children for us."

One after the other she described to him all the marriageable girls and tried to awaken his interest. But to no avail. He scarcely listened. He gazed at the clay and then at the jugs on the ground, and between his teeth muttered words that seemed to come from far away and tormented him.

Fatma attacked the subject again and only gave up when Afzal had absolutely refused all the girls in the village. Then she thought he must be suffering for love of a girl from somewhere else. Her insistence seemed to exasperate Afzal, who finally said:

"I'll marry the girl who will teach me to make singing jugs."

Bewildered by his words, Fatma nevertheless went from door to door asking if there were among the marriageable girls any who knew how to make singing jugs. The whole village talked about it, half incredulous, half captivated by the idea of singing jugs. But nobody could help her. Exhausted, Fatma set off home to her son who, she was beginning to believe, had gone mad. She had never heard of singing jugs, nor had Bassiri either she felt sure. Wherever had her son got the idea?

Halfway up the slope on her way back, Fatma heard a murmur behind her and turning, saw a growing crowd coming towards her along the road from the village. At their head came Om Hafiz, dragging by the hand a little girl with a garnet-coloured dress and flowing hair, too young to marry. Everybody seemed to be calling Om Afzal, so she stopped and Om Hafiz came up to her.

"I heard what you wanted," she said, "and this girl who lives with me says she knows the secret of the singing jugs. But she won't tell us. She will only tell Afzal. She's still too young to marry, but if your son learns what he wants from her, he will have to wait till she's grown up to marry her. Go and tell him."

The noise of the crowd had reached Afzal's ears and he appeared at the cottage door like a shadow. He beckoned the little girl to him and told everyone else to go away, including his mother. But nobody seemed to want to go: they were expecting all sorts of things to happen.

So Afzal took the little girl into the cottage and shut the door. In silence the villagers sat down by the roadside.

In spite of her self-assurance, the little girl was afraid when she saw Afzal so thin and pale and with such tired eyes. He only wanted one thing: to know the secret that would enable him to make singing jugs and rid him of the terrible nightmare.

"What's your name?"—"Asma," she replied. "Well, Asma, what is the secret?"—"Listen. When it was revealed to me in a dream I promised not to tell it except in exchange for another secret. So I'll tell you if you tell me how you knew that there were such things as singing jugs."

Afzal was impatient but was struck by Asma's air of sincerity and her courage. "A man told me that I should be able to make jugs that sing," he said, "if I mixed his bones with my clay. The man was drunk."

Asma believed him at once. "In my dream," she said, "there was a great cemetery with a lot of the graves marked in white. On each one there was a jug. You must go to the cemetery and get the caretaker to allow you to take the bones from the graves that are marked with white. You can grind them up and mix them with your clay. Then you can make your jugs and sell them as singing jugs."

"Where is this cemetery?"—"Come on," said Asma.

Afzal got out all his bags, threw them over his shoulder, opened the door wide and ran off after Asma, while the surprised villagers stood on either side of the road.

★　★　★

Afzal and Asma didn't have much difficulty in persuading the gravediggers to sell them the remains of the well-known drunkards who were buried in the cemetery. There were enough to fill three bags right to the top. Afzal bent under their weight, but the strength of his twenty years had come back to him with the hope of making the first singing jugs.

Back in the village, they went unnoticed, thanks to the darkness which had fallen. Tired of waiting, the villagers had gone home. Only Fatma was waiting for them, her head full of the strangest ideas. She really didn't know if her son was in his right mind, or if Om Hafiz had just wanted to get rid of the little girl. She consoled herself with the thought that the girl was too young to be any trouble yet and that Afzal would get out of it if Om Hafiz had deceived them.

As soon as he was home, Afzal set to work. Asma and Fatma helped him and did what he told them, grinding up the bones, mixing them with the clay and kneading it into a smooth mass.

The finished jugs were decorated and baked. Asma never left Afzal's home, but stayed there under the care of Fatma, who looked after her for the sake of the good she was doing her son. But Fatma was superstitious and felt uneasy about their visit to the cemetery. Afzal laughed and reassured her. He thought it was a wonderful idea and talked at length about his singing jugs, the sensation his discovery would make everywhere and his future wealth. He even spoke about his marriage to Asma.

★　　★　　★

A special cart was got ready to take the baskets of new jugs to the town. Afzal smiled proudly; the villagers stood at a distance and watched his preparations, but didn't dare to come up and buy one of the precious treasures that Afzal was expecting to sell for a good price to the rich townspeople.

Asma came with him and helped to push the cart over the rough places on the road.

When they came to the main town, Afzal in his former strong voice called out for customers: "Singing jugs, singing jugs!"

Very soon his cart was stopped and surrounded by passers-by wanting to know what it was all about. Afzal replied without hesitation that he had discovered the secret of making jugs that sang when anyone drank from them.

A customer came to buy the little red jug with the scalloped neck that lay on top of the others, but he wanted to make sure first that it really would sing. Asma went to the nearest inn to fill it and brought it back.

The customer had a drink, but the jug didn't sing.

Another customer tried it, but it still didn't sing.

They poured the water into another jug and tried that. It didn't sing either. They tried others, but without success. All the people there began to laugh and make fun of Afzal, while he grew paler and paler and looked more and more anxious. Asma was trembling. She trembled more for Afzal's sake than her own. If he beat her it wouldn't matter, but if he went mad and did something foolish, it would be her fault because her dream had encouraged him.

The situation was getting both sad and laughable. The rumour about singing jugs brought crowds of curious people from their houses and shops. But as soon as they got near, the laughter of the bystanders told them that everything was far from wonderful.

To cover her embarrassment, Asma went on shouting: "Singing jugs, singing jugs!", with such conviction that even Afzal, almost at the end of his tether, was struck. In the crowd a drunkard with a bottle in his hand pushed his way through the mass of people and from the cart grabbed the first jug that came to hand. He poured his wine into it and began to drink.

At once the jug started to sing a grape-pickers' song, and the silenced crowd listened in wonder.

41

THE WHITE CANARY

BEHIND BOZO'S PALACE stood the house of Soliman the Guard. Soliman had a daughter called Samira, whom he loved jealously. Samira's mother had died in giving birth to her and Soliman had vowed never to remarry but to live alone with his daughter.

Her father's gruff affection had made Samira a quiet, gentle creature with no pleasures or games other than the ones her father allowed.

Every evening before going to bed, Samira asked him to tell her one of the wonderful stories that he told so well, and in that way he always sent her to bed with a smile on her lips, dreaming of fairies and chivalrous princes.

The whole day long, Soliman guarded Bozo's woods and gardens and Samira was not permitted to leave the house for a single second. Nobody even knew that she existed. From early morning she was busy with the household tasks, preparing the meal for her father to cook when he came in, for he was so afraid that Samira would burn herself if she lit the fire.

She had her midday meal alone and sad.

Towards sunset her father came home, and through a gap in the hedge round the garden they would go off across the fields to gather vegetables and fruit for their meal. Samira loved the chance to caper about and feel the cool evening air on her burning face. She ran about till she was out of breath, hiding in the tall grass or behind bushes, making her father think that she had got lost, laughing and calling him at the top of her voice when she feared she had gone too far away.

43

For Soliman too, those walks and games were a great joy, but one which was partly spoiled now and then by some peasant going home late, or by one of Bozo's servants. When someone approached, he would call Samira with a sharp "Psst!", because he didn't want anyone even to know her name. They would go straight home, he with worry gnawing at his heart, she sulking over her spoiled outing.

★　★　★

When Samira was thirteen her father gave her a wonderful surprise. Near their home there was a small isolated pavilion which once must have been used for storing the gardeners' tools, but which was now empty. Soliman let Samira turn it into a spacious cage in which all sorts of birds were kept. Over two skylights was placed a lattice of small branches, and from wall to wall other longer branches were fixed and arranged in zig-zags, to let the birds flutter about as if they were in a tree. Stone bowls of water and seed were placed here and there and Samira was allowed to put a stool in the cage where she could sit and watch and listen to her new companions.

"Those friends aren't dangerous," said Soliman to himself, "they won't want to take my daughter from me; in fact, she will become fond of them and won't ever want to go away and leave me alone."

Samira wanted to have a lot of birds in the cage, but as it wasn't large enough several died, and she had to be satisfied with keeping only seven: a pair of doves, a pair of crows, a pair of hoopoes and a white canary.

Several times a day Samira went to see them. She took them their food, fresh water and leaves to cheer them up, but the birds kept away from her, suspicious and unhappy. In the evenings Samira would sadly and tearfully tell her father about them. She was hurt that the birds didn't trust her when she loved them so much, and Soliman didn't know how to comfort her.

One day Samira decided to set the birds free, as they weren't getting used to her. She went into their cage one morning, sat down on the stool and began to talk to them in her gentlest tones. "Little friends, I did so want you to love me. There are seven of you—one to brighten each day of the week—and you are the only creatures allowed to see me. I could have confided my sadness to you, but I am going to set you free. You will be able to go where I should have gone, out into the wide world, to look for the happiness that is everyone's right and that my dear father's jealous love denies me. I love you, but I feel I haven't the right to make you unhappy. Come, I'll open the door wide; fly away into the sunshine and the fresh air."

All the birds gave a flap of their wings and were about to soar skywards when the canary stopped them with a long shrill cry. It was a piercing call in which all Samira's pain poured out and went straight to the hearts of them all. It seemed as if the canary had caught the meaning of the girl's words and was expressing it in inspired cries for his fellow prisoners. He told them that this was their chance to do a good deed and that Samira had all sorts of nice things in store for them; she was such a kind girl for not wanting to keep them prisoners as she could have done.

And the door remained open to no effect. Each bird stayed where he was and flapped his wings without flying away, to show he agreed to stay.

Samira couldn't believe her eyes and went off leaving the door open, so that they could fly away after she had gone. But the canary kept on singing, telling the others how happy they would be if they stayed of their own free will and discouraging any impulse to escape. All night, instead of sleeping, he held them under his spell, and the next day Samira found them there, in spite of their empty bowls and empty stomachs. The canary had kept her friends for her by convincing them of the beauty of their prison. Samira's presence alone made it a paradise of trees and flowers, springs and sunshine.

Samira's joy knew no bounds. She called each bird in turn and gave him a grateful kiss. The canary refused her caress, and instead flew up into the furthest corner and huddled there. Samira called him in vain; he went on refusing and a blush showed through under his white feathers.

Every day she spent most of her time in the little room, looking after it and decorating it carefully. She didn't forget to bring the birds the best seed and fresh water. Then she would sit down and sing long heartfelt songs, which the birds listened to and seemed to understand.

And this is what she told them: "Since you are my friends, I can tell you my dreams; I am sure you will understand and be able to help me. Listen. I am no longer a little girl now that I am thirteen; so far I have only had the company of my father, who loves me dearly, it's true, but who doesn't understand my feelings. For him I must be an ever-present companion, always faithful and thinking only of him. He forgets that I am still very young and that I've seen nothing of the wonderful world that his stories describe. He tells me how much he loved my mother and I have to listen in silence. I have to keep from him my dream-love for a prince who will never come to find me in my quiet garden. I thought your company would change my life and that the care and affection I gave you would make me happy, and instead I feel my heart growing sadder. Now that I know you are prisoners for my sake and that even such different creatures can feel tenderness for me, I would like to be free to go in search of someone like myself who would love me as I love him."

And Samira put her head in her hands and sobbed. The birds fluttered about uneasily, not knowing what to do to soothe her. In pairs they put their little heads together and twittered their sympathy. The canary alone huddled up by himself, hiding his

46

beak among the feathers on his breast, as if he would burst with sorrow. Every time this happened the birds became fonder of the girl. In turn they would fly over to her, land on her and venture to kiss her. Samira stroked their heads affectionately in reply. But she was always surprised to find that the canary never followed the example of the others. She called him specially, holding out her arms as a perch and occasionally, so as not to seem too unfriendly, the canary came trembling to her and let her lift him up to her face. But suddenly he would turn his head away and it was always on the back of his white head that the kiss landed. Samira thought it all very strange and couldn't find any explanation.

When she left the cage, the canary would get into a state that alarmed his companions. He tried to sing words like those he had heard from Samira's lips. He made frantic efforts, but never managed to utter anything but incomprehensible cries.

After a fortnight he could pronounce "love", the word that Samira used so often, and he dreamed of the effect it would have on the girl the next time she came. But as soon as Samira was there the canary couldn't say a thing. The dove went up to him to encourage and urge him. But it was no good. The canary remained dumb. So the dove flew up to Samira and said "love" to her as naturally as anything. Samira thought it was magic and asked the dove to say the word again. The canary was furious and shouted instead "love, love, love, love", and flew onto Samira's shoulder. In wonder she listened to her canary friend saying over and over again "love, love, love".

From that moment Samira could teach her friends the language of her heart and every day the birds would repeat the sounds that came from her lips. The canary made tremendous progress. He even managed to make up speeches of his own, with the words of various sentences, which sent Samira off into dreams. He could talk of love in a surprising way, which would no doubt have won over any girl if she could have forgotten that he was a bird. His enthusiasm was boundless. He said things with so much ardour that Samira and her other companions wondered if it wasn't he who was their language teacher instead.

In spite of all this magic, Samira sometimes dropped back into her dejection and longed for young and handsome human beings with whom she could live and enjoy life. Then the birds were overcome with deep sorrow. What were they to do to make Samira happy? The canary got dreadfully upset and couldn't calm down. It was heartbreaking to see him.

He thought so intensively of her and her happiness that in inspiration one night he woke his companions. "Dear friends", he said, "we must do something. I suggest we go off to search for princes to bring back here for Samira to choose from. We'll go to the four points of the compass—I to the north; the two crows southwards; the doves to the west and the hoopoes east. We can use our language to persuade the princes from the neighbouring castles to come and see Samira. We must tell them that she is a princess who lives in Bozo's palace, and that they will be very happy if they marry her. Let's go straight away. Good luck!"

The two crows flapped away heavily towards the south. They hadn't understood very well what the canary had said, and they began to fly more slowly to talk it over. The female knew more about the problems of the heart.

"You know," she said to her husband, "our friend the canary is right to look for a prince for Samira. It's no good our singing or being affectionate, or even talking; we're only birds. I wouldn't have liked to be loved by a fox, and it's right that our mistress should prefer a prince to birds. The canary, who is more tender-hearted than we are, is more imaginative too, and he has sent us to find what he believes to be best for Samira among men: that is, a prince. Over there, in that great castle, we'll certainly find at least one and I shall be able to persuade him to come with us to

48

Bozo's palace. You'll help me, won't you?"

A few minutes later the crows, perched on the sill of an open window, were looking into a large hall the walls of which were covered with shining woodwork; in the middle stood a big table and round it twenty people were eating and drinking with great enjoyment. Behind each guest stood a lackey to fill his glass. At each end of the table sat men who seemed more important than the others, on account of their apparel and their more richly dressed lackeys. They were also emptying their glasses more quickly than the others, and their glasses were bigger. The two crows realised that these noblemen must be the lords of the castle, and that it was to them that they had to address themselves.

Without more ado, they darted to the two ends of the table and perched on the lords' shoulders, considerably alarming them. The lackeys, armed with their napkins, pursued and hit the frightened birds and chased them out of the windows.

The two crows were very miserable and perched in a tree in the garden to recover. What was to be done? To go back to Samira like that would be a terrible defeat. But how were they to reach those nobles who were defended by so many lackeys?

Meanwhile the meal was drawing to an end and the two princes, who were now quite drunk, had their servants conduct them to their apartments, where they ordered them to open the windows, for they felt stifled. What luck for our crows!

The two princes would soon be alone and the crows could approach them. The moment they were in bed, even before the lackeys had left them, the princes were sound asleep.

"Prince! My lord! Listen to us!" called the birds in vain. The two princes snored all the harder and heard not a thing. The two crows looked at each other in dismay and wondered what to do to wake them up and give them their message. The female crow suggested tickling them. With her beak at their ribs she did so

49

well that at last one of the princes was partly roused and, seeing the crow tickling him, imagined that a vulture was eating out his liver and began to shout for help, while the two crows, each in one of his ears, cried: "Prince, we have come to suggest that you marry the most beautiful princess in the world."

Extremely surprised to hear birds talking, and thinking he must be dreaming, he stopped calling and looked at his two magic visitors. They, taking advantage of the silence, repeated what the canary had taught them. The prince, wide awake now, loudly called to his brother, but shaking was needed to wake him up. They discussed the proposition.

"The princess in Bozo's palace!" said the one. "But she's been married for a long time! We asked for her hand twenty years ago! You must have made a mistake, Mr. and Mrs. Crow." "What is she like?" asked the other, who was even more drunk than the first and still half asleep. "She's the most beautiful princess that ever was, the sweetest and most affectionate; she has the hands of a fairy and an immense castle, and a great many more riches besides."

The two princes, who were more than fifty and so ugly that no princesses in the whole country had wanted to marry them, thought that this was not a chance to be missed. They called their servants and ordered a fine carriage for the morning, in order to go and visit the mistress of the talking crows and try to win her.

The male crow decided to wait and bring them, while the female went on to warn Samira and prepare her for the event.

This was done.

Samira, highly astonished at all the canary's plotting, refused to see the princes who were due to arrive at any moment. The crow begged for a long time, but to no avail. Samira would have none of it and even ordered the bird to go straight off to meet the carriage and stop it coming any further.

The bird set off and met the party not far from Bozo's palace.

The princes refused to turn back and kept the birds with them to make them show them the entrance to the castle. The crows, who usually saw Samira go out through the hedge when she went into the fields, knew no other means of access than the little door and led the carriage towards the opening. The princes thought all this very odd and became more and more annoyed. They hadn't rested all night and had drunk so much that their nerves were all on edge. Finally seeing that nobody was waiting to receive them, they resolved to take their revenge on the crows and began to pluck them alive. The crows cried out so loudly that the birds from all the woods in the neighbourhood came rushing; whereupon the princes let them go and gave orders to return home.

The poor crows went painfully back to their cage, not forgetting to thank their rescuers.

When Samira saw them coming in such a state, she was overcome with pity and wept and looked after them as she had never done before. She realised how much her friends must love her and what sacrifices they had made for the sake of her happiness. And suddenly too, she understood the tender-hearted little canary.

★   ★   ★

She was deep in thought when she saw the two doves arrive, out of breath and with their lovely white plumage covered in mud. For a long time they couldn't say a word.

In the cage, the two wounded crows, the two doves and Samira looked at each other in silence. "Dear doves," asked Samira at last, "where have you been, to get into that state?"

"Far away," they both replied. "We went to the green castle, where we thought we should find a prince for you."

Samira begged them to talk one at a time, but they both wanted to be the first to tell what they knew and it was impossible to understand anything. Samira picked up the male, stroked him and brushed the mud off, and he fell asleep. His mate told the whole tale of their journey all in one go.

"We set off first, towards the west, and were thinking of the green castle where we knew some princes lived. The canary had told us not to come back without a prince and we were sure of success. We were dreaming of seeing you with him, of going to your wedding and being able to say that you owed your happiness to us.

"But imagine how sorry we were when we got to the green castle and found a family whose children were scarcely a year or two old, and there was no prince for you. I suggested going further and looking for other princes in other castles.

"But alas, our troubles had only just begun! On the hills that surround the domains we had just left, we saw a hunting party galloping along, with noble lords on horseback in the lead. My husband decided that we should each choose ourselves a prince and pass on to him the message that the canary had entrusted to us.

"I immediately chose a handsome young man who rode so well that you would have thought he never did anything else. I imagined him at your side, beautiful mistress, and said to myself that nothing could be more splendid. I dived down and settled on his horse's back. 'Handsome prince, listen to me!' I called. The prince turned round and saw only me. He didn't understand. 'Good prince,' I said to him then, while he stared at me, 'will you listen to the loveliest story that I know?' Straight-way he took me in his hand and asked what I had to tell him. So I told him that Samira, Bozo's perfect little princess, would like to meet him and that she was the most beautiful of all the princesses in the world, with the most noble heart and a unique power: she could teach birds to talk, and I myself was a proof of her powers.

"Straightway the prince called to his companions that the dove he had in his hands was magic. The one who was holding my husband said the same, but my fine prince would have none of it. He firmly denied that there could be two such doves in the world and challenged him to make the bird he was holding in his hand say something. My husband, very proud to show his learning, repeated aloud the canary's teaching, and as it was very much like my account, my young prince was offended to find that the same proposal of marriage was being made to himself and to one of his companions. 'I'll be hanged if I believe you,' he shouted angrily, 'birds of ill-luck, chatterers and liars, trying to lead me into dangerous paths. I'll teach you to make fun of me; I'll give you to my dogs to eat.'

"For his part, the other hunter was likewise going to throw my poor husband into the gaping jaws of the pack.

"Realising the danger, I took advantage of a moment's inattention on the part of the prince to slip out of his fingers and like an arrow I darted upon the young man who held my husband. With a peck at his wrist I made him let go his grip and we were off at full speed.

"All the huntsmen were furious at being tricked, and rushed after us with their hawks, their arrows and weapons, while the dogs barked till the woods rang.

"We were in great danger and the odds were against us, for the great vicious hawks were capable of catching us and bringing us down. Taking advantage of our lead, I led the way towards a thick wood and sought the most bushy tree, in which to shelter our exhausted bodies.

"The hoarse cry of the dogs made us tremble right until night-fall, and every quivering of the foliage seemed to us the approach of a hawk. Heavy rain saved us, but since we couldn't take proper shelter, we were frozen. When it died down we were able to reach home. As we searched for something to eat in the fields, earth stuck to our feathers; and so here we are, dirtied and battered from all our adventures. But most of all we are sorry to have come back without accomplishing anything when success seemed so simple."

Samira listened to the story with heavy heart at the thought of those poor birds risking their lives to bring her happiness. She took the two doves in her hands, she warmed and brushed them, and showed her gratitude by singing them comforting songs.

She was just giving them something to eat and tending their wounds when she saw the two hoopoes coming.

★   ★   ★

They began talking straight away, without stopping for breath. "Eastwards, where the canary sent us, there is the sea, and as far as our wings would carry us we could find no prince at all. We want the canary to give us another region. We want to do something for you, dear mistress."

Samira thanked them for their kind intentions and their efforts. She told them that the canary hadn't consulted her before sending them on their wild adventures, which might have caused them all to lose their lives. She didn't want to marry a prince at all, since her father was only a guard at the palace. She was grateful to them, but she didn't in the least want them to risk their lives for her.

The birds took this for a reproach and were sorry they had been so quick to obey the canary, the smallest of them all, a mad thing who had led them astray by saying that their mistress's happiness was at stake. A fine thing if each one had brought a prince to the guard's little house!

In their hearts they were glad they hadn't succeeded.

They were so tired and aching that they said not a word more. Soon they were all fast asleep.

Samira wondered what had become of her little white canary.

★   ★   ★

Making straight for the north, the canary had flown over mountains and forests and at nightfall had stopped in a great oak tree near a large castle.

From where he was he could see into a dimly lit room. He went nearer and saw a young man lying ill. Round about him were doctors and his anxious family. Nurses came and went in silence and gave the patient medicines and pills.

For a moment the room was left empty and the canary ventured in. In the big bed, surrounded by magnificent hangings, lay the young man, who was scarcely breathing. He had a beautiful head and gentle eyes. He seemed to be only about fifteen, though in fact he was eighteen: his illness had weakened him so much that he had begun to look like a young boy again.

The canary liked him at once and said to himself: "That's the prince for my mistress; he's young and handsome like she is; he will love her as she deserves."

He flew lightly to the bed and perched on the cushion near the prince, who had just fallen asleep. He sang softly as if he were singing to Samira, and his pretty voice wakened the sleeper. With difficulty the prince turned his head towards the bird and stared at him as if to ask who had sent him to gladden thus the last moments of his life. The bird understood everything in his look and in a gentler voice than ever said to him:

"Dear prince, I've come to bring you happy news. From as far away as it's possible to come I have flown to tell you that my mistress, the beautiful, gentle, perfect Samira, has chosen you as her husband. If you could see her eyes, their goodness would cure you in an instant; the touch of her lips would give you the strength of a great oak; if you laid your head on her breast, the rhythm of her heart would quicken yours, and you would spend your lives in conquering the world. If you let her stroke your forehead, your fever and troubles would cease; if you placed your head in her lap, you would have the sweetest dreams; if, leaning

56

on her arm, you looked at the flowers, they would bloom more beautifully, the streams would sing and my brother birds, in admiration, would weave their flights about you.

"My mistress Samira transforms the whole world, nature obeys her and she changes everything into beauty. With her, the deserts are as meadows with abounding life. At evening, the stars drop curtsies to her; when she looks at the sky, the moon is always full, reflecting the light of her eyes. The finest pearls are humble on her fingers; her nails are perfect jewels. Every particle of her being is a mysterious shrine where the secrets of life can be discovered. Woe betide whoever dares to desire the whole inexhaustible treasure for himself alone: she was made to refresh thirsting worlds and, like cool fountains, her hands dispense happiness to all creatures.

"Prince, can you deserve this remarkable gift? Will you take the path of joy and exaltation and possess a universe of light? Can you love my mistress and draw strength from her for ever?"

"Canary, my friend," said the prince, "if life will remain in me, I promise you to do everything possible to deserve the providential gift that you bring me. I have never loved anything but your mistress's virtues. It is she, her sweetness, her power and beauty. It is she, her light, her glory and purity; it is indeed she. She may be called Samira, but I have always called her 'She'."

At that moment the door opened. The canary flew off without anyone seeing him. A nurse, who found the prince flushed and excited, thought he had had an attack of fever and ran for the doctors. It was no good their giving him medicines; he had been so quiet for so many days and now was in the grip of an agitation that nothing could calm. The doctors made grave predictions: "The prince will not last the night. This is the delirium that precedes death."

His parents came into the room, scarcely able to hide their grief. At each of the patient's vehement utterances, they forced back their tears, unwilling to believe that he was speaking the truth as he opened his heart.

★   ★   ★

The canary went and perched on a branch and looked at the horizon. Just then a particularly brilliant star was coming out and it seemed to speak to the canary. "Dear, kind-hearted bird, I will grant your dearest wish if for five evenings you will greet my appearance as you have today. You may trust my promise, for I am a powerful fairy."

And the star continued its course in the heavens, almost identical with the others. If the canary had stopped looking at it for a second, he would have had great difficulty in finding it again. But right through the night he studied it and followed it, to be sure of being able to find it again the next day. When it set, it signalled once more to him. He was deeply moved.

After that night spent watching the sky, the canary needed a whole day's sleep and he woke up just a few seconds before the star appeared. A special twinkling told him for sure that he was noticed and he heard a sound that seemed to say: "Two". He realised that the star was noting their second meeting.

How rich and blue and vast the sky was! The canary's soul was filled with its infinity, and he dreamed of Samira. She appeared against the majestic shining background, like a queen before whom a whole people bowed down. He mingled with the imaginary crowd and felt at one with their fervent feelings. So in contemplation he spent part of the night and woke light-hearted on the morrow to comforting sunshine.

★   ★   ★

The beautiful weather seemed ideal for exploring and our friend hurried away to the woods which surrounded the castle for several miles. He settled on the topmost branches, he dived earthwards, dizzy at possessing the space that no longer presented the slightest resistance to his body. He joined in the games of young birds, who accepted without alarm the stranger with the odd white plumage. He drank from all the springs, swayed on the smallest and highest branches alike and sang his conquest of the world.

He knew that all his joy came from the idea of Samira within him. He had no need to evoke her and recall her, the thought of her never left him. He found her in everything, in every creature, and the whole of nature that day seemed to acknowledge her and love her.

The weather was fine and everything was in perfect harmony. He thought of the young man who was ill and went back to the window. Calm reigned in the room. The prince was alone. Paler than a day or two before, he seemed much weaker. The canary flew up to him and landed lightly on his pillow, but the prince didn't move. So he sang out all his joy in a sweet and tranquil voice. As the prince seemed to rouse himself, the canary's song became more stirring. Without words he repeated his speech of the first evening, describing Samira. The young man, with little life left in him, nevertheless felt his cheeks grow more pink, and from behind his heavy eyelids he looked up wondering and questioning. The canary, modulating his voice, described in sweet music the emotions he felt every moment as he thought of Samira and the prince stirred out of his immobility. They began to understand each other more clearly. They were united in the same feelings of tenderness and both recognised that they were on the very road to happiness.

The canary sang for an hour and the prince fell asleep with a beautiful smile on his lips.

Once more when it was evening the canary waited for the star, silent and tense, wondering if his wish would really be granted.

The star appeared. The same twinkling as on the previous night counted: "Three".

★   ★   ★

The next day was very sad. The sky, heavy and threatening, no longer invited celebration and the canary sheltered from the rain under a cluster of branches. No bird dared to sing. Only the noise of the wind in the trees filled the air. "How shall I see the star?" said the little canary sadly and woefully to himself. "I only hope the wind sweeps the sky clear in time." The words came over and over again, like an obsession. He huddled up his little body as much as he could, into the smallest possible space, but his fear was great and seemed to stretch over the entire world. As a crowning misfortune, torrential rain began to fall. Hours went by; night came on with no change in the weather. The canary's heart beat so hard that he couldn't hear anything else. He was worried beyond measure. The poor little bird was no more than a tiny dot, lost in the darkness and filled with anxiety. Suddenly at the top of his voice he gave a heart-rending cry that startled all the inhabitants of the woods. Then, gathering his already failing strength, he darted skywards in the face of the torrential rain that beat against his wings. With an infinite effort, he went up and up till he broke through the thick, black, icy, menacing clouds. Thunder and lightning made the atmosphere more and more terrifying and the canary would have died of fright if the image of Samira had abandoned him for a single second.

As he came out of the clouds there rose up the star. "Brave little bird," it said to him, "you have only two more days of trial, then everything will be so beautiful."

The canary let himself fall back earthwards, his heart swelling with joy, forgetting all his efforts, the rain and the obstacles. A new song poured from his throat and was a strange sign for all the birds in the woods, for it was still raining and none of them dared to go out. For a moment, all their beaks poked out of their nests, but straight away went in again. Only the canary flew through the wood, indifferent to the floods that fell from the sky. Weary, he found a hole in a tree trunk, slipped in and immediately fell into a refreshing and well-earned sleep.

*   *   *

Sunshine and the songs of other birds greeted him gently when he woke.

He thought no more of the previous day's fears and struggles. It was a beautiful day and he wanted to live life to the full. First of all he had to go and tell the prince that his dream would soon come true. This time he found him very much paler, with his head sunk heavily into the soft cushions. The canary wanted to penetrate right to the prince's heart and make him realise that hope would soon become reality, that in two days and a night his troubles would be over. His song, soft at first, grew louder and faster, making the prince feel such exaltation that after several hours he gave some signs of life.

His cheeks took on a little colour. From the window the canary could see that the rhythm of his breathing was getting strong and steady like the rhythm of the song. His almost motionless eyes seemed about to open to the light. These signs encouraged the canary, whose aspirations rose to even greater heights, and in song he poured out the whole of his eagerness, to support the patient's efforts. But soon the prince became still again and the canary very sadly flew back to his branch.

Lost in meditation, he failed to notice that night was coming on and the stars appearing. He was grieved that he couldn't help the prince. Nevertheless, he felt an insistent tickling on the back of his neck, and turning suddenly, saw the star on the horizon. It was shining particularly brightly that evening, and he heard these words: "Canary, my friend, your goodness pleases me; you are doing all you can for your sick prince, who is scarcely of this world now. But tomorrow night you shall save him. Tomorrow I shall bid you goodbye; you will have fulfilled your pledge in every detail. And I shall keep my promise."

★   ★   ★

The canary, whose eyes were shining enough to light up the very night, rushed at once to tell the prince what he had just heard, but he found the window shut. He went back to his tree and stayed there the entire night, dreaming of Samira, who now had only one more day to wait for happiness. He imagined her in flowered dresses, laughing for joy and singing with him, running freely through the woods, picking flowers and making bouquets to give to everyone. Her former sufferings would disappear. In his dreams, Samira always appeared with her loveliest expression. The canary, thinking of her like that, stretched himself up on his little feet and felt nothing but her presence. The whole night long he dreamed this dream, and the star's promise kept coming back to him to encourage his imagination. He could hardly keep still.

The sun rose on a day of celebration.

It was the last day of his trial, and Samira was at last to be happy. This thought lent the canary new vigour and enthusiasm. He flew from tree to tree, waking the forest with his rich shrill song. The youngest of the birds followed him in a gaily coloured musical procession. He led them, climbing as high as he could above the trees, and diving down to the ground, skimming over streams in which their colours shone, and the delighted birds flew to and fro in joy of their own.

All by himself, the canary stirred up the entire population of the forest, and they, without knowing why, accepted the chance for rejoicing that seemed to have dropped from heaven. He went from one spot in the forest to another, inventing reckless games for the monkeys, races across the water for fisherbirds, and for the song-birds choruses and solos; new ways of swarming for the insects, and silent rhythmic marches for the worms. He didn't stop till all the living things in the forest had a share in his great delight and resounded in unison.

He drank a long mouthful of clear water and flew to the prince's bedside.

★   ★   ★

In his bed the prince lay pale and inert and seemed no longer living. In the canary's enthusiasm there was no room for heartbreaking reality and he said to himself: "I can breathe life into him."

"Prince," he said softly, "the time is coming when you will be strong and triumphant. I have set all the forest rejoicing for your wedding. Prince, gather up your strength. Not far from here, Samira is waiting to give you the loveliest heart in the world, like a great ruby created for your happiness. Do all you can to pick this pure flower; you must be capable of carrying out the task for which I have chosen you. If I were human I alone would be able to succeed. You must take my place. Beautiful Samira, the sum of all graces, is not only the most precious of creatures but also joy divine and perfect harmony."

Lost in praise of the girl, the canary didn't notice that a nurse had come in to tidy the room and had closed the window and the door.

Night was falling and the canary went on singing in the prince's ear. Suddenly he realised the time, flew to the window and knocked violently into it with his beak. Stifling a cry of pain he flew to the door, then to each corner of the room, seeking a way out. With each failure he became more and more agitated, and the darkness in the room increased. His last meeting with the star seemed finally prevented.

The window pane was too thick for him to break. His strength was failing and his heart beat as if it would burst. He flew to the prince, who hadn't stirred for three days. After trying in vain to make himself heard, the canary with his beak pulled at the sheets that covered the sick boy, but he made no movement. The canary needed so urgently to do something that he almost decided to peck the prince, but his heart bled to think of anything so cruel, and he uttered shrill piercing cries that expressed the extent of his anguish.

The high-pitched sounds woke the prince, who seemed to return from far off and not take in anything that was happening. The canary flew to him and in a cascade of sound, words and cries made him understand that it was absolutely necessary to gather what little strength he had left and open the window. The prince stirred in his bed, but so slowly that the canary was in despair. To help him, he began to sing a song into which he put all the courage he had and after a few moments that seemed to him centuries, the prince got up and dragged himself on frail legs to the window.

His slow feeble movements opened the window just enough for the canary to slip out, but the prince's effort cost him so much that he fell exhausted by the window, and died.

*   *   *

On his branch the canary caught sight of the star that appeared on the horizon and heard it say: "My noble courageous friend, go to Samira; she is waiting for you."

Forgetting everything else, with triumphant heart he sped off like an arrow towards Bozo's palace.

Halfway there he remembered he was still a bird and thought: "Ah, but what am I doing? I came to look for a prince for Samira and I'm going back alone. She will keep me in a cage, and

I shall see her still as unhappy as ever. No, that isn't what the star promised me."

He turned round and went back to the room where the prince lay on the floor pale and still.

The canary looked at him and said: "Prince, I will give my strength to your body, and my ardour to your eyes and human heart. You shall go to Samira and make her your wife. I will help you to love her as you must."

And putting his beak into the prince's mouth, with an immense effort and a feeling of profoundest joy he breathed out his life in one great stabbing burst of song.

*　　*　　*

His feathers and wings made a tiny heap on the floor, but the prince was on his feet and vigorously ringing a bell. A nurse answered, astonished at the unaccustomed tone, and seeing the prince with pink cheeks, walking about like a man in health and good spirits, she cried out that it was a miracle.

The prince talked to his family gathered round him with his doctors, who had no explanation for what had happened.

"Prepare a great feast for me; I am going away on my white horse to fetch Samira who lives in Bozo's palace. She will be my wife and we shall live together here. You will love her for she is the most beautiful and good and perfect of all the girls in the world."

Gathering up the canary's feathers, he held them affectionately in his hand, then placed them next to his heart.

He set off on his horse at a full gallop, and just as if he had travelled that road every day, went straight to Bozo's palace.

Samira was by the opening in the hedge. When he came up to her he said simply: "Come, mount my horse." And he took her away to his palace.

There they had prepared for him a sumptuous feast and the

prince's father sent his carriage for Soliman and invited him to live with them in the palace. Samira asked for her three pairs of talking birds to be brought and she settled them happily into her new home.

The marriage was celebrated the next day and everyone was full of admiration for the young people. But their greatest admiration was for the canary's little white feathers that had been placed in a crystal goblet.

Every year, for six days, the star fairy shines on the feathers and thus extols her faithful little canary. Then all eyes are dazzled and all those in love who dare to listen hear an irresistible song that assures them of happiness.

THE SNAIL SHELL

"Goodness, I'm tired!" said Go, the little snail, at the end of his trail.

He had climbed the six feet from the ground to the entrance of his home in blazing sunshine. And that grey wall was no joke, with its hollows and ridges and humps!

So as soon as he was indoors he got out of his shell, just like taking off a coat that makes you hot, and he relaxed in the shade with nothing on at all.

Everybody was asleep or pretending to be asleep and little snail Go, who would have liked to complain about the heat, had to be quiet. He couldn't even say that he was happy now, either.

The silence was catching and he too fell asleep.

He was suddenly woken by the noise of a quarrel. His two brothers were hurling abuse at each other and seemed about to come to blows. Go wondered why. He would so much have like to know! Softly he crept towards them. But it was too late. They were dealing each other dreadful blows with their horns and their mingled cries of anger and pain filled the house.

The whole family gathered round. Mother wanted to intervene. But the two combatants separated and, gesticulating wildly, knocked into Go's shell which rolled to the entrance and tumbled down to the foot of the wall.

At this catastrophe their cries ceased.

Not everyone had seen what had happened. But the two brothers realised all too well that the consequences of their fight were much greater than they had intended. Mother had seen the shell roll away. She turned round and saw Go quite naked. She realised what had happened and didn't know whom to scold. She laid the blame on Go, who for the moment didn't understand.

"It's your fault; fancy getting undressed at the front door! You ought to have been tidier and taken off your shell in your bedroom, beside your bed, like a well brought-up snail. It serves you right—and I'm going to give you a good spanking into the bargain."

Go, realising at last, gave way to despair. He wept and groaned and shouted, he wailed and called the God of Snails to help him, and broke everybody's heart.

Seeing such a flood of tears, Mother began to cry too and started to scold the two who had been fighting instead. "There's only one thing you can do now and that is go down and fetch the shell. It may not be broken. It may still be intact and not have been stolen. Even if it's a bit cracked bring it up. I'll try and mend it. I've got an old bit of grandmother's shell that I can use. Go down quickly before it's dark."

The two culprits crawled away in silence, hanging their horns. They soon climbed the six feet down, now that it was cooler and the path no longer hot from the sun. Once at the bottom, they searched among the grass and stones. In vain they struggled to lift big lumps; they found nothing, absolutely nothing. Not even a bit of shell dust!

Tired of searching, and with night coming on, they decided to go back home. Unwillingly. The thought of their mother's punishment and Go's tears was scarcely encouraging. They said not a word as they walked along, horn to horn, thinking sad thoughts.

But deep in thought, they lost their way and instead of reaching home found themselves suddenly, to their surprise, at the door of and unknown house. Its smell was quite different. But it was so dark. Perhaps there was a visitor who had brought his own scent with him.

Timidly they ventured in.

It was a snail's home and straight away the two brothers found a shell in their path. They felt it gently and since it was empty they had no doubt that it was Go's shell that someone had picked up and put there.

Their joy restored their spirits; with one flick of their horns they rolled it to the entrance without anyone seeing them and started to carry it home.

It wasn't easy It was already very dark. Besides, they had lost their way and they had to drag the shell which turned out to have a most inconvenient shape and to be terribly heavy.

At last, after immense efforts, they reached home in triumph.

At the sight of the shell they all forgot their worries. Even Go began to laugh and dance for joy. And as it was late, Mother gave the whole family something to eat and they all went quickly to bed.

It was scarcely daylight when they heard Go's cries once more.

Mother rushed out, fearing that the shell had fallen again. But a tearful Go met her: "It isn't my shell . . . mine was much more beautiful . . . it had white stripes and these are pink. And then, there were three bright spots. I daren't go in. There might be somebody inside!"

Very carefully Mother put her head through the opening: as far as she could see there was nobody inside.

"Try it all the same," she said to Go, "you can't be without a shell all your life, can you?"

Meanwhile the whole family had come running to examine the shell. It was obvious that it wasn't Go's. Everybody wondered about the other poor snail who must have lost his shell too. And the thieves were very sorry. But what could be done? Some of them said that the shell must be taken back. Then Go began to cry: it was better than having nothing. Since they had brought it, it was his and he wanted to try it. The rest agreed and, in order to avoid complicating the matter too much, they helped Go on with it.

Go had to get in backwards. Three snails held the shell. Go pushed with his hind-quarters, but they wouldn't go in. He was too fat. So Mother and his sisters started to push him. And they pushed and pushed, until quite a bit of his body had gone in. In the heat of the moment, however, nobody had heard Go shouting, and the poor thing had fainted!

They stopped pushing. They brought a little water and threw it over his face to revive him.

It was no use. Go had really had too much; he was almost suffocated. They could see his sides heaving as he tried to breathe.

Hastily they pulled him out. He came out more quickly than he had gone in. But his body was all hurt.

Poor Go!

Mother and his sisters stroked him and tried to bring him round. Father and his brothers were most unhappy.

It was terrible. What was to be done?

Go came to. He was pale and could hardly move. Every time he tried, he uttered a long drawn out "Ooh!" that broke their hearts.

They had to carry him gently to bed and look after him for several days.

When he was better, Mother suggested trying the shell again. But Go refused. He remembered the pain so vividly that he nearly fainted again. They didn't insist.

Nevertheless, Go wanted to go out for a little walk. Nobody dared to say no, so with one of his sisters on each side of him they started off. But on that rough wall it was impossible to crawl. With every movement, the tender skin on his body was torn, and Go bled. He went quickly back to his room and wept bitterly. Neither Mother nor his sisters knew what to do to comfort him. And his brothers felt guilty and sad.

Go thought he had better die. He ate nothing for several days and grew so thin that he hardly had strength enough left to lift his horns.

Then one of his sisters thought of bringing the shell and asking Go to slip inside. He hadn't the heart to refuse, and to please his sister he tried.

It was extremely easy now. The shell was even much too big for him. Go smiled a convalescent's smile and, puffing himself up to fill his shell, he set off.

He went right round the house, lifting his poor ears and cheering all their hearts.

That afternoon they had a party in the house.

Go ate so much that he didn't need to swell out to fill his shell any more. It fitted him like a dream; you would have thought that the good Lord had made it for him.

Mother suggested a walk.

The whole family set off joyfully to celebrate the happy day.

Everybody cracked jokes. Everybody was happy and looked at the sky with a fresh eye. Everything was beautiful. They were at peace with the world. Even the insects flying by within reach weren't worried.

Mother chose a lovely spot at the foot of the wall. It was quiet, and in the shade of the long grass they were sure of not being disturbed.

Go and his brothers danced and sang, lay on their backs and played lots of games, and the grown-ups watched them, happy to see them happy. They were almost feeling pleased with themselves over the lost shell which had brought them joy even after so many worries.

Suddenly a strong wind got up. The grass waved violently. And before the family could even think of taking shelter, something large and brown seemed to fall from the tallest of the blades of grass and came crashing down close to them.

When they had got over their fright they all looked in the direction from which death seemed to have threatened. What a surprise they had when they recognised Go's shell with its white stripes and three bright spots!

Go wanted to get out of his borrowed shell straight away and put on his own old one, but he couldn't. He had eaten too much, and his shell was holding him prisoner.

He begged his brothers to hold the shell while his sisters pulled him by the horns.

After great efforts Go was freed, all bruised again, with his horns hurting as much as his sides, and with his heart beating as if it would burst. He hadn't the strength to lift a horn and begged everyone to have patience for a bit.

Their high spirits were dampened.

Go was very worried. What would his shell be like? Was it better than the other?

All this time his brothers had been thinking of the other snail, the one whose shell they had stolen. "We're thinking that if Go goes back into his old shell," they said, "we must take this one back to its owner. Mustn't we?"

Mother answered thoughtfully: "I'm sure that those people where you took the shell must be very worried, like we were, and if they see you coming, instead of thanking you they'll punish you for what you've done. You might even be killed. You'd better not go."

They all thought it over. "We'll take it back," said one of the sisters. "Our brothers can tell us the way. When we get to the door we'll shout 'Who has lost a shell? We've found one'. Isn't that a good idea?"

"No," said Father. "Like us, they will already have looked everywhere and decided that the shell was stolen; so they will punish you just the same."

"In that case, we'll defend ourselves! There are four of us and we're in the right. They won't be able to do anything to us."

Mother was getting more and more worried at the turn of events and suggested that they simply take the shell back home. Go would then have a change of shell. They accepted that solution.

Go put on his shell as best he could. He felt uneasy inside it because of his bruises, but he didn't complain. His brothers carried the other shell back home.

That night Go didn't get a wink of sleep. He was worried and kept thinking of the other poor naked snail whose shell lay there useless. In his imagination he kept seeing another self wailing and suffering.

Go could bear it no longer. He went and woke his eldest brother and softly whispered his troubles in his ear. His brother was very sympathetic and, in spite of what his mother had said earlier, he agreed to take the shell back, with Go's help, to the house where he had got it.

He remembered exactly where it was and very very softly they dragged the shell back through the darkness to where it had to go.

Before they went in, Go begged his brother to examine the opening carefully and listen if anyone was awake. After some time he came back; all was quiet.

They slid quietly up to the opening and pushed the shell, being very careful not to let it roll. They left it right at the edge, but placed it firmly so it couldn't fall.

"I'd like to stay here till morning," said Go to his brother, "and not go home till I've heard the family's shouts of joy when they discover the shell."—"All right, let's wait," answered his brother.

The sun soon rose and from where he was Go could hear the household waking up. It seemed that they were suddenly making

74

a great deal of noise, but he couldn't make out what it was. "Let's go," said his wiser brother. "Supposing they come out to see if the people who brought back the shell are still here; they won't think we've done them a good turn; they'll want to punish us for stealing it."

Go agreed with him and off they went towards home. But Go was so weak that he couldn't go fast and, just as his brother had predicted, a lot of snails came hurrying in pursuit of them, shouting: "Stop thieves!"

They were big and strong and their anger lent them wings. "Listen, I'm the guilty one in all this," said Go to his brother. "Leave me and get home as fast as you can; go on. If I'm caught I'll try to defend myself and if Father and his friends will come to my rescue, tell them to be quick. I'll hold out as long as I can."

Taking advantage of his lead, Go's brother set off at full speed for his parents and told them everything. Everybody got ready to go and defend the noble little snail.

But Go had nevertheless had time to choose himself a nice little hole in the wall and climb into it. He retreated so far into his shell that nobody could get at him in any way.

His enemies approached. Soon they were there, angrily surrounding the hole and making an awful noise. The leaders realised how difficult it would be to get at Go in his trench and calmed their friends down. "Let's be absolutely quiet," they said. "He'll think we've gone away, and as soon as he comes out of his hole we'll catch him."

But Go had heard and didn't stir, waiting till his friends came to save him. Time went by. The aggressors grew impatient and some of them, disobeying their leaders, tried to push Go's shell and detach it from its hole. They pushed with might and main and Go hung on more and more firmly. But there were a lot of them and they were strong and pushed and pushed.

Go was at the end of his tether. He was just giving way when he heard, a short distance away, the war-cry of his parents and friends. He gained fresh courage and clung on desperately. The enemies left him and instead of trying to fight the oncoming snails, they took flight at top speed, scattering in all directions, pursued by the newcomers eager for battle.

Go's mother and sisters went up to him to revive him, for the tremendous effort he had just made had exhausted him and he had almost fainted. Go stuck his head out of his shell and smiled weakly at his parents. "You see," he said to them, "I did the right thing and so nothing serious has happened to me. I just couldn't have my shell back and leave some poor innocent thing to live without his. I suffered enough when I was naked; now that all's ended well, I shall be much more careful in future."

A little while later the whole family and their friends reached home. There had been no fight, the enemies having fled so fast that it had been impossible to catch up with them.

Go's mother invited everybody to a celebration and got out a lot of good things from her stores. They danced and sang and had a good time and afterwards Go very soon got better.

When he was grown up and had children of his own, he often told them the terrible adventure of the lost shell and all the dangers he had undergone.

His children were very sorry for him and they were never so unwise as to get out of their shells—even when it was very hot.

THE CHILDREN IN THE CLEARING

THEY HAD ALL met to go on an expedition: Tony, Leo, Andrew, Simon, Luke and Ronnie. They were all between seven and a half and eight and a half years old.

Tony was a strong boy, and he was the leader. They decided to go in single file, with Tony at the head, and they sang:

"His father will buy him a nice little trumpet,
 His father will buy him a trumpet of wood.
 Yes, his father has said so and so has his mother . . ."

And on and on they went.

Their way led them towards the wood and when they got there, Tony hesitated. "Don't be afraid," said Ronnie, the youngest. "In the story of Tom Thumb it says that if you drop white pebbles as you go along, there's no danger of getting lost."

But there weren't any white pebbles just there. So they began to collect yellow and red leaves which were easy to see. As soon as they had enough, they set off into the wood.

The trees were tall and covered with green leaves and birds of all colours flew from branch to branch singing gaily. The children looked up and tried to kill the birds with their catapults. But they didn't hit a single one. The birds flew off, still singing, just before the stones reached them.

Ronnie was dropping the leaves which were to guide them back again, putting a bit of dead wood on each one. Leo, who was walking along with his head in the air, fell into a bush and hurt his hands. They had to collect all their handkerchiefs to

77

make him bandages, dry his tears and blow his nose.

About midday they sat down to have their lunch and they emptied their haversacks almost entirely. "Now that my bag's empty," said Simon, "I shall be able to fill it with the birds that I'm going to catch."

"And if you don't catch any?" asked Tony.

"He'll fill it with stones," replied Andrew.

And they all laughed, except Simon of course.

Nobody managed to hit a single bird in spite of the great number of stones they fired. You would have thought that all the birds had agreed to make fun of them. It seemed as if they signalled to each other and warned each other when someone was aiming at them. And the children weren't at all pleased.

While they hunted, a strong wind got up in the forest. All the birds vanished in a hurry, making for the shelter of their nests. The wind blew and blew. The leaves made a strange sound, like a stormy sea. Branches creaked, and the old dry leaves and a good many of the seeds that had recently fallen were blown off the ground. Nearly all the leaves that Ronnie had put down flew away, in spite of the dead wood, and the children looked at each other in fright.

Luke began to cry: "I want Mummy. I want to go home. I want my Mummy."

But Leo scolded him straight away: "Aren't you ashamed! Crying before you even see if we can get out of the wood. Stop it. We've all got to keep quiet and try and find a way of getting out of here."

They sat down and put their heads between their hands. After a few minutes Tony declared: "I know. We'll stand all round a tree, with our backs to the trunk, and then walk straight ahead; we'll be bound to get out of the wood."

"No," said Ronnie. "One of us would get out perhaps, but

the others might all get lost. It would be better to stay together, wouldn't it?"

"Yes! Yes!" cried the ones who were frightened.

The children were silent. Only the wind still moaned.

"Does anybody remember how they taught us to find our way in the Cubs?" asked Andrew.

"Has anybody got a compass?" said Leo.

Nobody answered.

After thinking for a few minutes, Ronnie suggested putting together all the things that they had in their pockets, to see what could be done with them. Two penknives, a whistle, six catapults, three red matches and a few bits of string were all they found. No torch, no magnifying glass!

"What's left in your bags?" asked Tony.

"Some bread and an egg," said Leo.

"Nothing," said Simon.

"An orange," said Luke.

"Some bread, an egg and an apple," said Andrew.

"An egg and a bit of cheese," said Ronnie.

"I've eaten everything," said Tony. "And what about water; is there any left in your flasks?"

"Yes," they all said together.

And then they were silent again.

The wind had died down, but the sun was nearly setting. A few birds were singing in the distance. They seemed to be mocking them, glad to leave the children alone.

"Listen, all of you," said Tony. "We're going to camp out tonight, as if we were with the Cubs."

"Oh no!" said Luke. "My mother will be ever so worried if I don't go home."

"All right, go home," said Leo.

"How?"

"However you like."

"I'll stay then."

Tony ordered Andrew and Luke to make a space in the clearing; he sent Ronnie, Simon and Leo for some dead wood and he himself began to hunt for bits of wood that would catch fire easily.

A lovely fire sprang up, big, red and yellow. The branches crackled with a noise like a building collapsing. The children forgot everything and danced round it, singing. Tony knelt by the fire and kept it alight by throwing on little branches that were burnt up in a few moments. It was hot and the whole forest took on a red glow that delighted the children. Their shouts sounded just like Kipling's monkeys. You couldn't tell if they were singing or howling.

But what with the heat, and running round the fire, the day's worry and their tiredness, they dropped one by one to the ground and fell asleep. Tony himself, seeing them asleep, forgot he was the leader and followed their example.

So they slept without sentries for several hours.

★   ★   ★

The night grew cold. The fire didn't warm them any more; it had gone out some time ago. Oh! if only their mothers had been there! What would they have said, seeing their children lying there on the hard ground without pillows and blankets?

In the sky there was a little bit of a moon and a few very bright stars. But the children saw nothing because they were asleep.

Suddenly whistles could be heard, as if someone was being called. But the whistles were distinct, as if different people were calling at the same time. Then there was silence again. But soon a whistled song reached Ronnie's ears from a branch above him. It was so persistent that Ronnie woke up, without calling out or being frightened. And he listened.

He thought he heard a friendly voice saying to him: "Ronnie,

I've come especially for you. I've come to do whatever you ask me, but you can only ask for one thing. I've brought with me five of my friends to serve your five friends too. Only make sure you tell them that they can only give us one task each and it will be done without fail."

Ronnie got up and woke all his friends. They were all cross that he hadn't let them sleep and when he told them about what he had heard, they all said: "You've been dreaming."

Then from six branches six whistles sounded and six pairs of wings could be heard beating loudly.

"There!" said Ronnie. "You've frightened them away."

But the six birds weren't going away; they flew down to the children's feet and let them stroke them. And each boy began to think about what he would ask for. "We'll wait until the first wish is granted," said Tony, "before making our wishes. You begin, Ronnie."

Ronnie asked his bird to go home and bring him back his torch and handkerchief, which were under the pillow on his bed, and his penknife from the table.

The bird set off at once and reached Ronnie's house.

Doors and windows were shut. So the bird dived into the chimney and came out in the dining room. The whole house was silent. It flew ever so quietly, so that the sound of its wings shouldn't disturb anyone. Fortunately the door of Ronnie's room was ajar and it was able to slip through and up to the bed without a sound. The sheets got all black from the soot that its wings had picked up in the chimney. With its beak it turned the pillow over, picked up the handkerchief and placed it round its neck, took the torch in its beak and hopped onto the table to look for the penknife. No penknife. Ronnie had made a mistake. So the bird shook a pair of trousers hanging in the open wardrobe and the penknife, which was in the pocket, fell to the ground with a noise that resounded in the dark. The bird slipped a claw

through the ring on the penknife and dragged itself to the chimney. With one flap of its wings it was out and flew away to the wood.

Its arrival was greeted with shouts of joy. The children had lit another fire, and they all danced round it with the birds.

Ronnie took his things. His handkerchief was all black and there was hardly any light left in the torch. Ronnie's hands got all black too and he asked his bird to get him some water; but it flew up onto its branch.

"It's my turn now," said Simon. "Now what can I ask the bird for? I know—I'll ask it to go to school and open my desk and do my sums for me."

His bird flew off at once and came back some time later to perch on its branch. Simon wondered if it had done as it was asked.

Tony asked his bird for something to drink. Immediately the bird came back with a jug filled with such cold water that you could only drink a few drops of it at a time. The bird held the jug by its handle and gave some of the water to Tony and all those he pointed to. They all drank some of the water and it quite took away their thirst, although they had been very thirsty indeed.

Then Andrew said: "I should like my bag full of fruit, so that when I get back Mummy won't be cross."

His bird flew straight off, and a few seconds later Andrew was bombarded with fruit falling from the sky. He filled his bag, and there was still enough left for everybody to have two things to eat then and there. Then his bird went and perched on its branch.

Leo hesitated. "I'm going to make the most of this chance," he said. "I want my bird to bring me something that my parents can't afford. So I'd like that satchel, the one that costs so much, in the window of the 'School Outfitters'."

His bird came back a minute or two later with the satchel he wanted and Leo proudly put it on his back, after carefully examining the inside where he found everything he had longed for.

Luke was just about to ask for goodness knows what when he thought of his mother and began to cry: "Mummy, Mummy, I want my Mummy!"

So the bird, which thought that that was his wish, began to peck his bottom so hard that Luke ran away. The bird followed him, or rather drove him in the direction of his home. When the other children saw what was going on they ran after Luke, and in that way all managed to get out of the wood.

*   *   *

It was already getting light. Luke's bird wouldn't leave him alone. It pecked him as soon as he stopped. When they were nearly home, the bird flew away and the children turned round to see where it was going. Then they noticed the six birds flying together, very high up, and they waved their handkerchiefs to them. The birds swooped down to place a little blue stone on the shoulder of each child and said: "That's to comfort you." And the saddened children watched them fly away.

Their parents, who had been out searching for their children and who had had a very worrying night, came up just then.

They were extremely happy to see their children safe and sound. They ran up to kiss them. Holding them in their arms, they forgot their anxieties and the weariness of the night. They asked dozens of questions: "Were you cold?"—"How did you spend the night?"—"Are you hungry?"

And they all took their children off home.

But once they had calmed down, the parents got together to decide what they were going to do, because they had to show those children that their escapade in the forest was very naughty, and that naughtiness must be punished.

The parents' meeting lasted two hours. It was decided that the children should be kept indoors for two days, without seeing any of their friends.

The children were told of their decision. They didn't understand at first, but they had to obey. Some hours later, each one thought to himself as he stared out of the window: "Our parents are funny; they were so happy to have us back alive; they were so pleased to be able to give up the search and not to have to worry any more—and now suddenly they decide to punish us. And to punish us for what? For not being dead? For not getting hurt or not coming home ill? Really, they are funny!"

In their minds' eyes the children went over the whole adventure. What had they done wrong? Going for a walk, going hunting in the wood with some friends? It wasn't the first time. Was it their fault if they had got lost? And wouldn't it be more understandable for their parents to try to console them rather than punish them?

It was no good the poor children wondering; they couldn't understand their parents. But they loved them so much that each one had a nice idea.

Each of the six in his own room, at the very same time, got the little blue stone out of his pocket and instead of asking for comfort asked for his parents to be shown the whole story of their expedition.

And there in the midst of their work the fathers and mothers saw the whole of their children's adventure like a film. The parents stood surprised and fascinated right up to the last movement of the last bird which had brought the children out of the wood.

Leaving their work, they ran to their children to tell them how sorry they were for not understanding, and asked them to forget their punishment. All the parents thought they had had a vision which explained the truth about the children's adventure, and none of them suspected that the same story had been seen by the others.

When the children got together again they were astonished to find that they had all had the same thought at the same time, and they thanked their friends the birds.

When the parents were alone they told each other what they had seen. They all talked at once, not knowing that the same vision had appeared to them all. When they knew what had happened, it was one more reason for believing the truth of the story which was talked of for years in that part of the country.

MADCAP IN THE CLOUDS

"Daddy! Daddy!"

Mary's voice came from the bedroom. Her father ran in and looked everywhere for her. She wasn't hiding under the bed, or in the wardrobe, or behind any of the furniture.

He stood perplexed in the middle of the room, wondering if he really had heard Mary's voice.

He was just about to go out of the room, thinking he had been mistaken, when a shower of beans fell on his back.

Surprised and cross, he turned round.

There before his eyes, dancing on top of the wardrobe, was his little daughter Mary.

"Mary, Whatever are you doing? How did you get up there? What have you done with the ladder?"

"I didn't use a ladder; I jumped up here from the floor," she replied.

"What! You jumped? That's impossible. You're making fun of me."

The words were hardly out of his mouth when Mary jumped onto his shoulders and stood there. Afraid she would fall, her father caught hold of her legs, but Mary slid down and sat on his shoulders.

"Really, you must have gone mad," he said. "I shan't call you Mary any more, but Madcap."

Mary gave a leap onto the bed, rolled over and ran off.

Her father told her mother what had happened, and they both decided that from then on everyone should call Mary "Madcap".

Perhaps that would teach her to stop these latest tricks.

*   *   *

Of course, Madcap wasn't embarrassed by her name. In fact, it amused her, and every day she found new ways of living up to it.

She had soon jumped up onto all the cupboards in the house and cleaned off the dust that had accumulated there. But what she liked most of all was discovering boxes and all sorts of things that her mother kept up there. She had collected twenty-three boxes like this, which she put in her room. She had put something into each one, and that kept her busy for a long time.

But soon she found that it wasn't such fun any more, just jumping onto cupboards and cleaning them, so she opened the door of the flat.

The door led onto the landing. Madcap looked over the bannisters at the four floors between her and the ground floor. Suddenly she wanted to slide down the bannisters, as she had seen the boys do so often.

Her mother would certainly have forbidden it, but she had such confidence in her muscles and knew she was so light that there was no danger.

So she climbed onto the bannisters and let go. She felt so much at home there that she soon began to do tricks. She turned round as she slid and sat astride the bannisters, or lay on her tummy, with her feet and hands in the air. She clapped her hands and had a marvellous time.

When she was nearly at the end of her slide she had gathered so much speed that she got ready to fly. She spread her arms for wings and stretched out her feet like a rudder.

And out she sailed through the main entrance. She flew over the dense traffic that filled the street just then, and ended her flight in a basket of apples in the greengrocer's shop opposite.

Madcap was so light that not a single apple fell out.

She had hurt herself a little; but as she did not want to be caught by the shopkeeper or the passers-by, she didn't make a sound but jumped quickly out of the basket.

Standing by the wall, she looked at her house and saw her mother knitting on the balcony.

"I wonder if she saw me?" thought Madcap. "I don't think so, because she would have called me back and scolded me. I'll give her a surprise by climbing up the drain-pipe at the side of the balconies."

Madcap walked across the road just like anybody else, avoiding the cars and buses.

Once on the pavement outside her house, she realised that the passers-by would see her climbing up the drain-pipe and would certainly stop her.

She decided it was better to jump. In four leaps she went from balcony to balcony till she got to the one where her mother sat.

Her mother, hardly expecting a visit of that sort, was alarmed and called out before she noticed that it was her own little girl there before her.

It was lucky she didn't faint. What would Madcap have done with a mother all pale, lying on the balcony floor? And with no-one to help her?

But Mother recovered a little. To see her daughter quite calm and smiling after causing her such a fright made her angry.

She scolded the thoughtless little girl so much that she cried bitterly, and instead of going to her bedroom or saying she was sorry, Madcap gave a leap and landed on the roof.

Up there she went on crying. She couldn't see why her mother scolded her.

★　　★　　★

For a moment, she stopped crying. Through her tears she saw two large hawks hovering above her head. She forgot her tears and dreamed of joining these birds who kept themselves up in the air with such ease, gliding like the flying carpets in stories.

When she thought they were close enough, she gave a jump and landed on the back of one of the hawks.

In spite of Madcap's lightness, the bird took fright, flapped his wings and soared up into the sky like an arrow.

Madcap was all the while in danger of falling but, cleverly following the hawk's movements, she kept her seat on his back so well that the bird almost thought he had grown a hump and slowed down once he reached the safety of the clouds.

A sea of mist surrounded Madcap and the bird. She couldn't see a yard in front of her. In a second, the little girl's dress was damp and clung to her like a swimsuit.

But the bird went up and up to get out of the clouds. As soon as he was above them, Madcap jumped from his back and landed on the white cloud that they had just left. Beneath her feet, like thistledown, there stretched an immense grey-white carpet. Only a little girl as light as Madcap could walk on it.

In her hands she gathered up vapour as you do snow; she pressed it together to make a bed, then she lay down and looked at the sky.

Oh, how different the sky was, away from the town! The sun was very warm, but she could almost look straight at it if she closed her eyes a little. And there were the stars. In the town, nobody could see them during the day. Madcap gazed in wonder at the world that her mother had never told her about. It seemed to her that just by stretching out her arms she could pick up stars and make herself a necklace of light. But she was lazy and only dreamed of it.

After a while she felt quite rested and wanted to go for a little walk on her cloud.

But where could she go? No streets, no gardens, no friends to visit, no houses.

So Madcap decided to break from the big cloud a smaller one like those she used to see from her window.

She stretched out her leg and with it drew a big circle.

Fortunately the wind was blowing the right way at that moment and the circle of cloud that Madcap's leg had cut out came away from all the rest and floated farther off.

She was on an island. She watched as the cloud where she had rested so long got further and further away, and she saw too that there was sky on both sides of it. The hole she had made for her island had disappeared. It was just as if she hadn't made it.

For a little while yet she looked round about her, and it was only then that she felt herself the owner of a desert island.

What was she going to do?

There's nothing to do on a cloud.

But had she gone such a long way up just to be bored?

Madcap sat down on the edge of the cloud. She felt in danger of falling so with her hands and feet she arranged her cloud in the shape of a basin, with a parapet almost up to her chest. Like that it was safer.

She asked the stars if they wanted her to dance for them, and it seemed to her that they sparkled with delight at the idea.

And Madcap began to dance. Round and round she went, pointing her toes and doing all the steps she had learned on earth. She felt she needed a veil to add grace to her movements, so she bent down as she danced, gathered up a bit of cloud and with it made a delicate transparent scarf.

She danced and danced and wanted never to stop. She grew dizzy with movement and didn't notice that some big birds had come and perched on the parapet of her island.

There, admiring her, were an eagle, a vulture, a cormorant, a few falcons and some hawks, all round the dancer.

When Madcap fell tired onto her velvet carpet, the birds applauded, clapping their wings.

Then she noticed they were there, and waved gracefully to them. As their eyes met hers, each in turn politely bowed his head.

After a few minutes' rest, during which everything was perfectly quiet, Madcap got up and sat on the edge of the cloud facing the eagle.

She felt at ease in their company and the birds seemed to be paying homage to the wingless queen who had come all alone to their realms.

Madcap wanted to get to know her new friends. First she spoke to the eagle:

"Tell me, Friend of the Sky, who sent you to me?"

"Shall I tell you, enchanting creature, that my path ought to have taken me far from you, that I ought to forget the delight of watching you and look for food for my children in the mountains? But you are so graceful, Friend from the Earth, that my duty to my children could not stop me coming to thank you for your visit."

Madcap, looking into the eagle's eyes, understood all he had said and didn't know what to answer.

She left her seat and, dancing round, came back to the eagle and stroked his head. The cloud trembled as the eagle quivered with suppressed delight.

Next, Madcap stopped in front of the vulture.

"And what were you doing here, while I was dancing for the stars?"

The vulture hid his hooked beak with his enormous wing and said nothing. He hid his face in shame, for he dared not tell the innocent little girl that he was looking for carrion.

Madcap thought he was shy, and went on so as not to embarrass him.

Next, she looked at the cormorant.

"I was off on my long daily journey in search of food," he said without waiting to be questioned, "but when I saw you dancing more gracefully than a holy bird, I said to myself: 'you'll fly ten times faster presently; stop a moment now.' And then it didn't occur to me to set off again. Shall I stay near you all my life? Dance for me for one minute each day, and I'll run all your errands in the sky."

Madcap didn't know what to reply; she couldn't take such a big bird home. Mother would be so frightened. But he was so nice and gentle, in spite of his curved beak!

Finally Madcap said she would try and talk to her mother about it. She would write him a reply if he would give her his address.

The cormorant was very touched and didn't answer.

The hawks and falcons spoke in chorus:

"We are the birds that fly over towns and we recognised you, daughter of men; we came to you as we were going towards your houses in search of food, but we have become like our children, who still receive everything in their beaks. We are enthralled by your beautiful dancing. Will you dance again?"

So Madcap did another little dance, a completely new dance that she made up especially for her admirers. And the more she danced, the more firmly the birds held on to the cloud; it seemed they never wanted to leave her again.

But no matter how much Madcap wanted to please them, she was too tired and hungry to go on.

She thought of home; memories of the food she liked returned and she remembered her mother. It occurred to her that mother had probably been very unhappy since she left, and Madcap wanted to go back to the world of people.

Using both hands, she dug a hole in the middle of the cloud, to look at the earth. The birds thought she was getting ready to do a new dance, but she lay down on the cloud and looked through.

94

She was so high up in the sky that it was difficult for her to see the bottom of the hole. But gradually she was able to make out the blue of the sea.

Madcap trembled with fear. How far away from her house she must be! However could she get back? And what would Mummy and Daddy do without their daughter?

She got so frightened that all the birds wondered what to do to calm her down. The cormorant, who was used to making long journeys, was the first to speak. "But we are here" he said. "All strong-winged princes of the heavens. Command, and we shall obey you."

Madcap was comforted by these words and told them that she wanted to go back to the place she had come from.

But where was it? How can you see where you are in all that blue?

The eagle said they would harness themselves to the cloud and pull it here and there until Madcap recognised where she was.

So off they went, the strongest in the middle, the others at the side, flying so fast that even the wind blew the other way when it met them.

In a few moments they had gone miles and Madcap, all the time watching at the edge of the hole, recognised the green country, the hills and rivers of her own district. "Just a little further, friends, and we shall be over my house."

But as they neared the town, the big birds who avoid mankind left the cloud, flew over Madcap's head, stroking it with their wings, and soared into the blue of the sky.

The hawks, who stayed till last, pulled the cloud round till it faced the earth and sped off to their nests far away in the hills.

Madcap was left all alone as her cloud sailed on towards the centre of the town. Nobody dreamed she was there. Her heart beat faster at the thought of seeing her parents again.

"They must have been dreadfully hurt when I went away;

they will have looked everywhere without finding me. But when they have me back they will be happy again, I'm sure."

Impatiently she ran from her hole to the edge of the cloud and back again, to see whether she was getting nearer home.

There were the streets below her already and she could hear the buses and the car horns. More and more impatient, she drew a spiral in the cloud with her outstretched foot, from the middle towards the edge. When it was finished, Madcap picked up the central end of the spiral in her hand and jumped through the hole into space. And the cloud unravelled slowly, like a skein of white wool on the end of which hung the little girl.

When the whole cloud had unravelled and only the tightly-packed edge she had made remained in the air like a hoop, driven along by the wind, Madcap managed to put her foot down on the telephone wires. To keep her balance more easily, she pulled the cloud down and broke off a piece to hold in her outspread hands like a tightrope walker.

The whole street was full of people staring in bewilderment. But Madcap didn't worry about them; she slid along the cable to reach her house as quickly as possible.

In all the streets she passed over, the balconies and windows and shop doorways were already crowded with people. The cars and buses stopped and people got out of them to watch the little girl sliding so fast along the telephone wires.

All the spectators waited tensely for her to fall. But Madcap was so light and agile that she went from one street to the next along the cable just as if she was walking on the ground.

When she got to the street where her own house was, she waved to her parents who had come out onto their balcony too. They didn't know that it was their daughter, but they very quickly recognised her.

She heard their voices calling out to her to come home straight away, saying that they would forgive her everything and that they still loved her.

So Madcap, using the piece of cloud as a sail, gave a big jump and flew down to her parents, who received her with open arms.

Everyone clapped such a clever jump. Madcap waved both hands to the people in the street and blew kisses to them.

Daddy and Mummy wanted to look at their daughter and rejoice at having her back at last.

They went into the sitting-room and asked Madcap to tell them about her adventure.

But Madcap was hungry.

They gave her all the nicest things in the house but couldn't let her finish a mouthful, so impatient were they to know the whole story.

At midnight Madcap was still telling them about her journey and her eyes were closing with sleepiness.

The next morning Daddy asked Madcap not to give them such terrible frights any more and not to go up so high in the clouds again. Wasn't it enough for her to jump onto trees and houses?

Madcap promised to be careful and always to tell her parents where she was going.

Madcap's father sent her to dancing lessons and by the time she was twelve years old she was already the best dancer in the world.

THE MAGIC FOREST

NARA WAS A VILLAGE of woodcutters and a great forest nearby had always provided for all its wants.

In a corner of the forest, high up on the hillside, were some very strange trees. No-one dared touch them. The foresters used to say that anyone who tried to cut them down would have bad luck; but why this should be nobody knew.

One day some young woodcutters, all about twenty years old, decided to visit this part of the wood and examine the trees more closely. So they sent out one of their number as a scout.

Three days went by and he didn't return.

The others were worried and decided to go into the wood and find out what had become of him.

They got to the hill-top and there, at the edge of the trees, they found their friend's body, covered with cotton wool. They went closer and found that he had tried to cut down one of the trees; but as it was made entirely of cotton wool, it had fallen at the first stroke of the axe, right on top of the woodcutter, and had smothered him.

What a strange forest, where trees were made of cotton wool!

Going further into the wood, the four woodcutters saw a smaller tree and to find out what it was made of they threw their axes hard at it; but the blades of the axes broke as soon as they struck it.

"Ah!" they said. "Here is a tree that is harder than iron; fancy such a small tree being so hard! This really is a strange forest."

They examined the tree more closely and found that it was

99

made of black diamond. No tool was sharp enough to cut it.

Next they came to a third tree which was as large as an oak, and wondered what it could possibly be made of. Naturally, they didn't dare to touch it. One of the young men suggested that they should scrape the bark and when they did so they saw that it was made of copper. To make sure, one of them struck the tree with his axe, with all his might. A long spark flashed from it and, striking the woodcutter's shirt, set light to it. Terrified, he rushed back to his companions, who put the fire out with their jackets.

Everyone was now quite frightened so they decided to go straight home. But on the way the oldest of them had an idea.

"Since we were brave enough to come here," he said, "why don't we bring a few visitors to see this strange place? It would certainly provide some amusement." The others agreed and the very next day they suggested to their neighbours a visit to a place where no-one had been before.

About fifty decided to go, so they arranged to visit the strange trees again the next Sunday.

When the day came all the people in the party, except the three guides, thought they were going for a walk simply to enjoy themselves. Nobody suspected in the least that the trees had already cost one woodcutter his life, that they could break axes and set shirts alight! So they sang as they climbed the hillside.

When they got to the top, one of their guides asked them if they wouldn't like to chop down this great bushy tree. It wasn't the copper tree. However, fearing some surprise, the guide gave each man an axe with a very long handle and asked them to stand as far back as possible from the tree while they worked. They were all to strike at the same time.

"One, two, three, go!" he cried.

Then the great tree, just as it was, broke away from its roots and floated straight up into the air. It was made of silk, and the tear made by the axes had let the air in and caused the tree to fly away.

In astonishment everyone watched as the tree flew through the air, blown this way and that by the wind. They found it hard to believe that so large a tree could be so light, and they craned their necks to see it as long as it was visible. At last it disappeared in the clouds on the horizon.

Much amused by this adventure, the visitors and their guides chose another tree. It was greyish in colour and of medium size, and from its branches hung thousands of leaves all shaped like tiny bells, and pink flowers in the form of bigger bells.

The guide who had been burnt wasn't at all happy.

Before letting the visitors strike the tree he scratched the bark. Immediately the leaves began to ring out, making an extraordinary clamour. Cling! Cling! Clang! Clang! went all the leaves together. It went on and on and seemed as though it would never stop. Everybody covered their ears, but it had no effect; on the contrary, the noise seemed to grow louder. Some ran away, almost driven out of their minds by the monotony and volume of the sound.

The guide struck the tree again, hoping that this might stop the noise. The leaves stopped moving, but the flowers started to ring instead; but their music was so pure and lovely that everyone lay down on the grass and listened entranced.

Soon sleep overcame them all, and only one man, older than the rest, was able to resist. He walked up to the tree and placed both hands against its trunk. The music stopped.

If he hadn't done so they would all have been kept asleep by the lullaby till they died of hunger. Going from one sleeper to another, he woke them all and advised them to leave the enchanted wood then and there.

The wisest agreed, but the younger ones still wanted to stay, hoping to discover some more of the secrets of the forest.

So they split up, some returning to the village and others going in search of another tree which might offer them some amusement.

They noticed a shining, cylindrical tree, with its branches climbing to the sky in a spiral. So they got ready to cut it down.

But at the first blow of the axe the tree fell down on top of them and covered everyone with the layer of sticky paper which formed its bark. The people struggled to get out of the paper, making holes in it with their hands and heads. Their feet tore more holes but the sticky bark stuck fast to their clothes and bodies in strips. A pointed branch, as tall as a chimney, fastened itself to each one's head; two others, straight and thick, attached themselves to their chests and backs to complete the comic effect. Even their arms had a little branch. They couldn't help each other, not being able to get close enough; as soon as one tried, a jab from another's branch made him give up.

"How can we get back to the village like this?" they asked. "The old people will laugh at us; the children and dogs will run after us. What a fix! Curse this forest! Why were we so curious?"

"We can't stay like this. We've got to eat and sleep."

"Let's stay here until tonight, and then go back when everybody is in bed. Our mothers and sisters are sure to help us."

"Yes, but we might trip and fall in the dark; we must go now."

So they started off straight away.

When they got near the village they separated, to avoid people's jeers. Each one went into his home by the back door, signalling to his mother without attracting his father's attention.

When the mothers saw the change that had come over their sons they couldn't help crying. Their handsome sons, reduced to such a state!

It was impossible to get the tightly sticking bark off without lots of boiling water, and the ten young men were so badly scalded that they had to stay in bed for a month.

By this time, all the village knew that the forest was dangerous and that it was best not to go into it. Every night mothers would warn their children as they put them to bed never to go near it, or something dreadful would surely happen to them.

★   ★   ★

The son of the village carpenter, who was twelve and whose name was Ray, was the leader of a gang of six children; they always did what he told them and followed him in everything.

One evening, when they met just outside the village, Ray suggested a visit to the forest. They all promised not to do anything silly, and to do whatever their leader said without arguing. They had to be careful not to be caught, for their parents would never have forgiven them for being so foolish, especially after so many warnings.

They set out first thing next morning. When they got to the wood they looked carefully at all the trees, taking care not to touch them or go too close. As they were looking carefully all round they noticed in the middle of a clearing an enormous tree whose branches grew very high up. Spaced out on the trunk there were holes just big enough to take a foot or a hand.

"I think this tree is all right," said Ray. "Look, it's asking to be climbed. Pass me the saw and chopper, Andy. I'm going to climb up."

So he began to climb, with the chopper in his belt and the saw slung across his shoulders. Up and up he went, while his friends waited with bated breath for the order to follow him.

When he reached the place where the branches started, Ray suddenly missed his step; but a branch leaned down and helped him regain his balance.

"Yes, this is a friendly tree," he shouted down. "Come on up, everybody."

And up they all scrambled. In two seconds they were each sitting on a strong branch, looking down on the valley. How proud they felt to have been the first to discover a tree that didn't do anyone any harm!

"I wonder what this tree can be made of?" asked Ray.

"Gold," replied Ginger.

"What! Gold?"

"Yes. I looked through a hole in the bark and it's gold."

"Gold, Ginger? Are you sure?"

"Yes."

"Everyone get down," said Ray. "I'm going to try and cut a branch off. If the tree kills me go straight back home. If everything is all right, everybody will get something."

Then slowly Ray started to cut off a branch with his saw. After a lot of hard work the branch gave way and fell. The children all shouted: "It really is gold."

Ray went on to another branch and cut off seven pieces. They were small enough to be hidden under jackets, and the children each took a piece home. They said nothing to their parents, who had forbidden them to go to the forest, and hid the gold branches in a corner of the garden.

The next day they went to the forest again, meaning to uproot the golden tree. They dug a hole round the trunk, but the more they dug, the deeper the tree sank into the ground, so that after an enormous struggle they had to give up the idea altogether.

"The tree is stronger than we are," said Ray. "But it's a good tree, and we must obey it. Let's go home."

No sooner had he spoken than a branch fell at his feet, making a sound for all the world like "Thank you."

On the way back home again, Ray told his friends that they musn't say anything about their golden branches, and that they must never take more than a tiny piece of gold each day to buy what they wanted.

And the next day, two of the children, each with a piece of gold no bigger than a nut, went to the baker's for some cakes, and tried to pay him in gold.

"But, my young friends," said the baker, "with that amount you can buy enough to eat for a whole year; I can't give you enough change."

When the children had gone, the baker rushed off to their parents and told them what had happened. He asked the parents if the children hadn't stolen the gold from them; but they answered that they had never had any. They wondered where the children could possibly have found it. The fathers and mothers of all seven children got together to find a way of making them tell their secret.

But the children had been ordered not to tell anyone and so, despite blows and promises, their parents didn't find out anything. There was nothing to it but to watch the children day and night till they gave themselves away.

For two whole months the parents of the seven children watched in vain. Then one day Clo, the youngest, couldn't resist the temptation to go and have a look at his branch so at midday, thinking that his parents were busy and out of the way, he dug it up.

His father, however, had been watching him from the doorway and came running out towards him. Before Clo could hide the branch his father seized it, smiling with pleasure.

Clo began to cry and begged his father not to do anything, or his leader would be angry with him. But his father was far too happy at discovering the secret of the gold. He knew now that a tree in the magic forest had those precious branches and he refused to listen to Clo.

He called his friends together and said to them:

"Our children have discovered a golden tree; are we going to be foolish enough not to take advantage of it? We must make them show us where it is, so that we shall make no mistake."

Ray's father ordered him in front of all his friends to show him the golden tree in the forest. Ray, who knew how to make himself obeyed, could obey too and so all the village went off towards the forest.

When they reached the tree Ray said:

"Here it is."

Everybody looked but saw nothing. Only the seven children could see the tree.

Ray's father came over to him. "Where is it?" he said.

"Here it is."

"Ray! Stop making fun of me."

"Why, Dad! Can't you see it?"

"No, I can't. And I'll teach you to make fun of me. There!"

And he boxed his son's ears.

The other children cried out indignantly: "But there is the tree!"

As they all pointed to the same place, Ray's father realised that the tree must be invisible, but no-one could understand why it should be visible to some and not to others.

"Climb it, Ray."

So Ray climbed it again, just like the first time, and everyone watched him climbing in the air, without seeing the tree. He seemed to be raising himself up into the air, into space; and everyone's mouth fell in astonishment.

When he got to the top Ray called out: "Well, father, what shall I do now?"

"Cut a branch and throw it down."

Ray sawed off a branch and let it fall. As it did so, it touched the arm of one of the men, who called out excitedly:

"I can see the tree! I can see it! How big and beautiful it is! Quick! I'm coming up."

Ray sawed off other branches and all those who touched them were able to see the tree.

When there were fifteen of them they became so impatient to get the treasure that they told Ray to come down and climbed the tree themselves; they placed ropes round the roots and looked for a small tree on which to fasten the ropes that would pull the big tree over.

As soon as they began to pull, the small tree burst open, spilling a great quantity of syrupy-smelling liquid over the ground. The bees and all other insects in the forest, attracted by the syrup, came in such numbers that the noise of their wings deafened everybody.

The villagers didn't know what on earth to do, whether to run away from the threatening insects and abandon the tree, or to put up with the bites and have the gold. Some went, but there were still enough left to tug at the tree.

They changed the direction of the ropes and pulled with all their might. The tree began to lean, and they cried: "Hurrah!"

But the more the tree leaned, the smaller it became; and when it was lying on the ground it was no bigger than a stick a few inches long.

The woodcutters were so disappointed that they didn't know what to say.

Then Ray spoke. "Pull the other way," he said. "Perhaps the tree will grow large again."

Sure enough, as they pulled the tree upright it became its original size again until, when it was upright, it was as large as ever.

"Are those branches enough?" asked Ray.

"Yes," answered the older ones.

"Well," said Ray, "when you want more, the tree will give you them willingly."

Hardly had he finished speaking when several branches fell at his feet, and he gave them to everyone who was there.

They returned to the village and decided to follow Ray's advice, and for three hundred years the people of Nara received from the tree enough gold to live on in plenty.